Book of Lists

The Homeowner's Book of Lists

Judi Kesselman-Turkel and Franklynn Peterson

Contemporary Books, Inc.
Chicago

Published by Contemporary Books, Inc.
180 North Michigan Avenue, Chicago, Illinois 60601
Manufactured in the United States of America
Library of Congress Catalog Card Number: 81-66082
International Standard Book Number: 0-8092-5853-6 (cloth)
0-8092-5856-0 (paper)

Published simultaneously in Canada by
Beaverbooks, Ltd.
150 Lesmill Road
Don Mills, Ontario M3B 2T5
Canada

Other books by the editors:

Author's Handbook
Magazine Writer's Handbook
Good Writing
Eat Anything Exercise Diet (with Dr. Frank Konishi)
Handbook of Snowmobile Maintenance and Repair
The Do-It-Yourself Custom Van Book
How to Improve Damn Near Everything Around Your Home

By Judi Kesselman-Turkel:

Stopping Out: A Guide to Leaving College and Getting Back In

By Franklynn Peterson:

Children's Toys You Can Build Yourself
How to Fix Damn Near Everything
The Build-It-Yourself Furniture Catalog
Handbook of Lawn Mower Repair

Contents

Note: Lists, charts, estimators, and other useful information contained in *Homeowner's Book of Lists* are arranged alphabetically, with most charts on similar topics grouped together. To help you find other related listings, a Cross-Reference Guide is included at the end of the book.

An Invitation

Even though we scoured the shelves of major reference libraries, hounded corporate keepers of information, and pored over millions of pages of government documents, we must have missed *some* useful lists. If you want to see the next edition of *Homeowner's Book of Lists* include some of the lists you have been looking for but haven't found, drop us a note about them. Better yet, if you come across some lists that you would like to see included in *Homeowner's Book of Lists,* send them along. (Be sure to let us know the lists' sources, such as name and date of the magazine or book you took each one from or the company that printed the list.) Thanks!

Franklynn Peterson
Judi Kesselman-Turkel
c/o Contemporary Books Inc.
180 N. Michigan Avenue
Chicago, IL 60601

The Homeowner's Book of Lists

Baking ingredient substitutions

1 tablespoon flour (for thickening) = ½ tablespoon cornstarch (approximately)

1 cup sifted all-purpose flour = 1 cup + 2 tablespoons sifted cake flour

1 cup sifted cake flour = 1 cup minus 2 tablespoons sifted all-purpose flour

1 teaspoon baking powder = ¼ teaspoon baking soda + ½ teaspoon cream of tartar

1 cup milk = 3 tablespoons sifted nonfat dry milk + 2½ teaspoons margarine, or ½ cup evaporated milk + ½ cup water, or ¼ cup sifted dry whole milk powder + ⅞ cup water

1 cup buttermilk or sour milk = 1 tablespoon vinegar or lemon juice + enough sweet milk to make 1 cup (let stand for 5 minutes) or 1¾ teaspoons cream of tartar + 1 cup sweet milk

1 cup cream, sour, heavy = ⅓ cup butter + ⅔ cup milk in any sour milk recipe

1 cup molasses = 1 cup honey or 1¼ cups sugar + ¼ cup liquid

10 miniature marshmallows = 1 large

1 ounce chocolate = 3 tablespoons cocoa + 1 tablespoon fat

1 cup corn syrup = 1 cup sugar + ¼ cup liquid

1 tablespoon active dry yeast = 1 package active dry yeast or 1 compressed yeast cake

1 whole egg = 2 egg yolks, or 3 tablespoons + 1 teaspoon thawed frozen egg, or 2 tablespoons + 2 teaspoons dry whole egg powder + an equal amount of water

1 egg yolk = 3½ teaspoons thawed frozen egg yolk or 2 tablespoons dry egg yolk + 2 teaspoons water

1 egg white = 2 tablespoons thawed frozen egg white or 2 teaspoons dry egg white + 2 tablespoons water

Source: *About the House: New Ideas for Easy Management from Bissell,* © 1977 by Dorison House Publishers, Inc.

Bed linen sizes to buy

Bed description	Mattress size (approximate inches)	Suggested flat sheet size (inches)	Suggested blanket size (inches)
Sofa bed, bunk, or rollaway	30x75	54x90 or 66x96	66x90 or 54x80
Studio bed	34x75	54x90 or 66x96	66x90 or 54x80
Single	36x75	66x96	66x90
Twin (regular)	39x75*	66x96	66x90
Twin (extra-long)	39x80*	66x96	66x90
King-size twin	42x80	81x102	66x90 or 80x90
Three-quarter-size	48x75	81x96	80x90
Double sofa bed	52x75	81x96	80x90
Double (full)	54x75*	81x96	80x90
Double (extra-long)	54x80*	81x102	80x90 or 90x108
Queen	60x80*	90x102	90x108
King	76x80*	102x108	90x108

*Fitted sheets are commonly supplied in these sizes.

Birdhouse dimensions

Species	Size of floor	Depth of cavity	Entrance above floor	Diameter of entrance	Height above ground
	(Inches)	(Inches)	(Inches)	(Inches)	(Feet)
Bluebird	5x5	8	6	1½	5–10
Robin	6x8	8	*	*	6–15
Chickadee	4x4	8–10	6–8	1⅛	6–15
Titmouse	4x4	8–10	6–8	1¼	6–15
Nuthatch	4x4	8–10	6–8	1¼	12–20
House wren	4x4	6–8	1–6	1–1¼	6–10
Bewick's wren	4x4	6–8	1–6	1–1¼	6–10
Carolina wren	4x4	6–8	1–6	1½	6–10
Violet-green swallow	5x5	6	1–5	1½	10–15
Tree swallow	5x5	6	1–5	1½	10–15
Barn swallow	6x6	6	*	*	8–12
Purple martin	6x6	6	1	2½	15–20
Prothonotary warbler	6x6	6	4	1½	2–4
Starling	6x6	16–18	14–16	2	10–25
Phoebe	6x6	6	*	*	8–12
Crested flycatcher	6x6	8–10	6–8	2	8–20
Flicker	7x7	16–18	14–16	2½	6–20
Golden-fronted woodpecker	6x6	12–15	9–12	2	12–20
Red-headed woodpecker	6x6	12–15	9–12	2	12–20
Downy woodpecker	4x4	9–12	6–8	1¼	6–20
Hairy woodpecker	6x6	12–15	9–12	1½	12–20
Screech owl	8x8	12–15	9–12	3	10–30
Saw-whet owl	6x6	10–12	8–10	2½	12–20
Barn owl	10x18	15–18	4	6	12–18
Sparrow hawk	8x8	12–15	9–12	3	10–30
Wood duck	10x18	10–24	12–16	4	10–20

*One or more sides open.

Source: *Homes for Birds*, U.S. Department of the Interior.

Birds' favorite plants

The following are lists of trees, shrubs, and flowers that provide natural shelter and choice seeds for birds of various species.

Annual flowers

Abelia
Aster
Blessed Thistle
Buddleia
California Poppy
Centaurus
Cosmos
Forget-Me-Not
Love-Lies-Bleeding
Marigold
Portulaca
Princesfeather
Princesplume
Rockpurslane
Sacaline
Silene
Sunflower
Tarweed
Zinnia

All of these will attract seed-eating birds, such as cardinal, goldfinch, sparrow, chickadee, nuthatch, titmouse, and towhee.

Trees

Beech—titmouse, towhee, blue jay, cardinal.

Black Cherry—mockingbird, robin, towhee, vireo, finch, flicker.

Flowering Dogwood—woodpecker, kingbird, waxwing, cardinal, catbird, bluebird, brown thrasher, purple finch, robin, towhee, vireo.

Hackberry—brown thrasher, mockingbird, robin, flicker, cardinal, bluebird.

Holly—catbird, bluebird, brown thrasher, waxwing, mockingbird, flicker, robin, thrush.

Juneberry—bluebird, cardinal, catbird, flicker, scarlet tanager, thrush.

Mountain Ash—catbird, cedar waxwing, flicker, robin.

Mulberry—cardinal, thrush, cuckoo, oriole, waxwing, vireo, warbler.

Oaks—blue jay, grackle, crow, woodpecker, brown thrasher, nuthatch, titmouse.

Pines—chickadee, nuthatch, warbler, titmouse, grosbeak, brown thrasher, blue jay.

Red Cedar—bluebird, sparrow, robin, flicker, mockingbird, purple finch, cardinal.

Sassafras—catbird, flicker, robin, towhee, vireo.

Sour Gum—purple finch, waxwing, bluebird, robin, towhee, flicker, brown thrasher.

Alder, ash, birch, and elm—seeds are attractive to many birds.

Shrubs

Althea (rose of sharon)—hummingbird, goldfinch, sparrow, downy woodpecker, nuthatch.

Bayberry—catbird, chipping sparrow, thrush, junco, song sparrow.

Blackberry—vireo, oriole, sparrow, woodpecker, thrush, towhee, catbird.

Blueberry—robin, titmouse, chickadee, waxwing, cardinal, tanager, phoebe.

Elderberry—woodpecker, indigo bunting, chat, kinglet, phoebe, cardinal, towhee.

Pokeberry—bluebird, cardinal, robin, mourning dove, flicker, towhee, catbird.

Privet—waxwing, catbird, thrasher, robin, mockingbird.

Pyracantha—waxwing, brown thrasher, mockingbird, robin, bluebird, finch.

Snowberry—thrush, grosbeak, bobwhite, robin, cedar waxwing.

Spicebush—cardinal, catbird, robin, vireo.

Sumac—bluebird, brown thrasher, flicker, hermit thrush, mockingbird.

Viburnum—bluebird, finch, thrush, waxwing, flicker, robin.

Winterberry—bluebird, brown thrasher, cedar waxwing, hermit thrush, purple finch.

Vines

Virginia creeper, greenbrier, honeysuckle, trumpet vine, wild grapes—towhee, finch, vireo, woodpecker, bluebird, robin, sparrow, catbird, mockingbird, cedar waxwing, hummingbird.

Source: *Attracting and Feeding Birds,* Fish and Wildlife Service, U.S. Department of the Interior.

Canning and freezing yields from fresh fruits

Food item	Purchasing unit* (Net weight)	Approximate yield, canned (Quarts)	Approximate yield, frozen (Quarts)
Apples	48 lb. (bushel)	16–25	16–20
	44 lb. (box)	14–23	14–18
Apricots	48 lb. (bushel)	12–24	30–36
	22 lb. (crate)	6–12	14–17
Berries (except strawberries)	36 lb. (24-qt. crate)	11–24	16–20
Cherries, as picked	56 lb. (bushel)	22–32 (unpitted)	18–22
Cranberries	25 qt. (box)		
Grapes	48 lb. (bushel)	12–20	
	18 lb. (12-qt. basket)	5–7	
	28 lb. (lug box)	7–8	
	20 lb. (4-basket crate)	5–7	
Peaches	48 lb. (bushel)	16–24	16–24
	20 lb. (lug box)	7–10	6–10
Pears	50 lb. (bushel)	17–25	20–25
	46 lb. (western box)	15–28	18–23
Pineapples	70 lb. (crate)	12–16	28–35
Plums	56 lb. (bushel)	22–36	19–28
	20 lb. (crate)	8–13	6–10
Rhubarb	10 lb.	7–10	5–8
Strawberries	36 lb. (24-qt. crate)	7–16	19-30

*Legal weight of a bushel of fruit varies from state to state.

Source: *Handbook of Food Preparation,* American Home Economics Association.

Carpet fiber performance ratings

Fiber	Durability	Crush recovery	Soil resistance (oil base)	(water base)
*Wool	Excellent	Excellent	Good	Fair
†Nylon	Excellent	Excellent	Good	Fair
‡Polyester	Very good	Very good	Fair	Excellent
◦Acrylic	Good	Very good	Fair	Very good
•Olefin	Very good	Poor	Good	Excellent

*More expensive than man-made fibers.
†Longer wear than wool of comparable quality.
‡Soft and luxurious underfoot.
◦Looks and feels much like wool.
•Not damaged by moisture.
Source: *Selecting a Carpet*, University of Maryland Extension Service.

Carpet padding performance ratings

Type of padding	Feeling underfoot	Recommended weight (ounces per square yard)	Recommended thickness (inches)
Sponge rubber	Bouncy	48–64	Minimum ¼
Rubberized hair-jute	Firm	40 (moderate traffic) 50 (heavy traffic)	¼ (moderate traffic) ⅜ (heavy traffic)

Source: *Selecting a Carpet*, University of Maryland Extension Service.

Carpet pile density performance ratings

Pile density (tufts per inch)	Durability	Crush resistance	Texture and appearance
3–4	Fair	Fair	Sparse; backing may show
5–6	Good	Good	Medium-thick
7–8	Very good	Very good	Dense, thick, and luxurious

Source: *Selecting a Carpet,* University of Maryland Extension Service.

Carpet texture performance ratings

Texture	Durability	Crush resistance	Resistance to shading	Resistance to matting	Ability to hide dust
Level loop	Excellent	Excellent	Excellent	Excellent	Fair
Multilevel loop	Very good	Excellent	Excellent	Excellent	Very good
Cut and loop	Very good	Excellent	Excellent	Good	Very good
Cut pile					
Low twist	Very good	Fair	Poor	Poor	Fair
Medium twist	Very good	Good	Fair	Fair	Fair
High twist	Very good	Very good	Good	Good	Fair
Frieze	Excellent	Excellent	Very good	Excellent	Good
Shag	Good	Poor	Excellent	Fair	Excellent

Source: *Selecting a Carpet,* University of Maryland Extension Service.

Cheese varieties' characteristics

Kind or name (Place of origin)	Kind of milk used in manufacture	Ripening or curing time	Flavor	Body and texture	Color	Retail packaging	Uses
Very hard ripened varieties							
Parmesan (Pär´-mē-zăn´) also called Reggiano (Italy)	Partly skimmed cows' milk	14 months to 2 years	Sharp, piquant	Very hard, granular, lower moisture and milkfat than Romano	Creamy white	Cylindrical, wedges, shredded, grated	Grated for seasoning in soups, or vegetables, spaghetti, ravioli, breads, popcorn, used extensively in pizza and lasagne
Romano (Rō-mä´-nō) also called Sardo Romano, Pecorino Romano (Italy)	Cows' milk; in Italy, sheep's milk (Italian law)	5 to 12 months	Sharp, piquant	Very hard, granular	Yellowish-white interior, greenish-black surface	Round with flat ends, wedges, shredded, grated	Seasoning in soups, casserole dishes, ravioli, sauces, breads, suitable for grating when cured for about one year
Sapsago (Săp´-sä-gō) (Switzerland)	Skimmed cows' milk	5 months or more	Sharp, pungent, cloverlike	Very hard	Light green by addition of dried, powdered clover leaves	Conical, shakers	Grated to flavor soups, meats, macaroni, spaghetti, hot vegetables; mixed with butter makes a good spread on crackers or bread

Kind or name (Place of origin)	Kind of milk used in manufacture	Ripening or curing time	Flavor	Body and texture	Color	Retail packaging	Uses
Blue-vein mold ripened varieties							
Blue, spelled Bleu on imported cheese (France)	Cows' milk	2 to 6 months	Tangy, peppery	Semisoft, pasty, sometimes crumbly	White interior, marbled or streaked with blue veins of mold	Cylindrical, wedges, oblongs, squares, cut portions	Appetizers, salads, dips, salad dressing, sandwich spreads, good with crackers, dessert
Gorgonzola (Gôr-gŏn-zŏ′-lă) (Italy)	Cows' milk; in Italy, cows' milk or goats' milk or mixtures of these	3 to 12 months	Tangy, peppery	Semisoft, pasty, sometimes crumbly, lower moisture than Blue	Creamy white interior, mottled or streaked with blue-green veins of mold, clay-colored surface	Cylindrical, wedges, oblongs	Appetizers, snacks, salads, dips, sandwich spread, good with crackers, dessert
Roquefort (Rōk′-fĕrt) or (Rôk-fŏr′) (France)	Sheep's milk	2 to 5 months or more	Sharp, slightly peppery	Semisoft, pasty, sometimes crumbly	White or cream white interior, marbled or streaked with blue veins of mold	Cylindrical, wedges	Appetizers, snacks, salads, dips, sandwich spreads, good with crackers, dessert
Stilton (England)	Cows' milk	2 to 6 months	Piquant, milder than Gorgonzola or Roquefort	Semisoft, flaky, slightly more crumbly than Blue	Creamy white interior, marbled or streaked with blue-green veins of mold	Circular, wedges, oblongs	Appetizers, snacks, salads, dessert

Soft, unripened varieties							
Cottage or low-fat cottage (Unknown)	Skimmed cows' milk, cream added	Unripened	Mild, acid	Soft, curd particles of varying size	White to cream white	Cup-shaped containers, tumblers, dishes	Salads, with fruits, vegetables, sandwiches, dips, cheesecake
Dry curd cottage (Unknown)	Skimmed cows' milk	Unripened	Mild, acid	Soft, curd particles of varying size	White to cream white	Cup-shaped containers, tumblers, dishes	Salads, with fruits, vegetables, sandwiches, dips, cheesecake
Cream (U.S.A.)	Cream from cows' milk	Unripened	Mild, acid	Soft and smooth	White	3- to 8-oz. packages	Salads, dips, sandwiches, snacks, cheesecake, desserts
Neufchatel (Nû-shä-tĕl′) (France)	Cows' milk	Unripened	Mild, acid	Soft, smooth, similar to cream cheese but lower in milkfat	White	3- to 8-oz. packages	Salads, dips, sandwiches, snacks, cheesecake, desserts
Ricotta (Rĭ-cō′-ta) (Italy)	Cows' milk, whole or partly skimmed, or whey from cows' milk with whole or skimmed milk added. In Italy, whey from sheep's milk	Unripened	Sweet, nutlike	Soft, moist, or dry	White	Pint and quart paper and plastic containers, 3-lb. metal cans	Appetizers, salads, snacks, lasagne, ravioli, noodles and other cooked dishes, grating, desserts

Kind or name (Place of origin)	Kind of milk used in manufacture	Ripening or curing time	Flavor	Body and texture	Color	Retail packaging	Uses
			Firm, unripened varieties				
Gjetost (Yēt´-ôst) (Norway)	Whey from goats' milk or a mixture of whey from goats' and cows' milk	Unripened	Sweetish, caramel	Firm, buttery consistency	Golden brown	Cubical and rectangular	Snacks, desserts, served with dark breads, crackers, biscuits, or muffins
Mysost (Müs-ôst) also called Primost (Prēm´-ôst) (Norway)	Whey from cows' milk	Unripened	Sweetish, caramel	Firm, buttery consistency	Light brown	Cubical, cylindrical, pie-shaped wedges	Snacks, desserts, served with dark breads
Mozzarella (Mō-tsa-rel´-la) also called Scamorza (Italy)	Whole or partly skimmed cows' milk in Italy, originally made from buffalos' milk	Unripened	Delicate, mild	Slightly firm, plastic	Creamy white	Small round or braided form, shredded, sliced	Snacks, toasted sandwiches, cheeseburgers, cooking, as in meat loaf, or topping for lasagne, pizza, and casseroles
			Soft ripened varieties				
Brie (Brē) (France)	Cows' milk	4 to 8 weeks	Mild to pungent	Soft, smooth when ripened	Creamy yellow interior, edible thin brown and white crust	Circular, pie-shaped wedges	Appetizers, sandwiches, snacks, good with crackers and fruit, dessert

Camembert (Kăm´-ĕm-bâr) (France)	Cows' milk	4 to 8 weeks	Mild to pungent	Soft, smooth, very soft when fully ripened	Creamy yellow interior, edible thin white or gray-white crust	Small circular cakes and pie-shaped portions	Appetizers, sandwiches, snacks, good with crackers, and fruit such as pears and apples, dessert
Limburger (Belgium)	Cows' milk	4 to 8 weeks	Highly pungent, very strong	Soft, smooth when ripened, usually contains small irregular openings	Creamy white interior, reddish-yellow surface	Cubical, rectangular	Appetizers, snacks, good with crackers, rye or other dark breads, dessert
			Semisoft, ripened varieties				
Bel Paese (Bĕl Pä-ā´-zĕ) (Italy)	Cows' milk	6 to 8 weeks	Mild to moderately robust	Soft to medium-firm, creamy	Creamy yellow interior, slightly gray or brown surface sometimes covered with yellow wax coating	Small wheels, wedges, segments	Appetizers, good with crackers, snacks, sandwiches, dessert
(Brick) (U.S.A.)	Cows' milk	2 to 4 months	Mild to moderately sharp	Semisoft to medium-firm, elastic, numerous small mechanical openings	Creamy yellow	Loaf, brick, slices, cut portions	Appetizers, sandwiches, snacks, dessert

Kind or name (Place of origin)	Kind of milk used in manufacture	Ripening or curing time	Flavor	Body and texture	Color	Retail packaging	Uses
Muenster (Mün´-stẽr) (Germany)	Cows' milk	1 to 8 weeks	Mild to mellow	Semisoft, numerous small mechanical openings; contains more moisture than brick	Creamy white interior, yellow tan surface	Circular cake, blocks, wedges, segments, slices	Appetizers, sandwiches, snacks, dessert
Port du Salut (Por dü Sa-lü´) (France)	Cows' milk	6 to 8 weeks	Mellow to robust	Semisoft, smooth, buttery, small openings	Creamy yellow	Wheels and wedges	Appetizers, snacks, served with raw fruit, dessert
				Firm ripened varieties			
Cheddar (England)	Cows' milk	1 to 12 months or more	Mild to very sharp	Firm, smooth, some mechanical openings	White to medium-yellow-orange	Circular, cylindrical loaf, pie-shaped wedges, oblongs, slices, cubes, shredded, grated	Appetizers, sandwiches, sauces, on vegetables, in hot dishes, toasted sandwiches, grating, cheeseburgers, dessert
Colby (U.S.A.)	Cows' milk	1 to 3 months	Mild to mellow	Softer and more open than Cheddar	White to medium-yellow-orange	Cylindrical, pie-shaped wedges	Sandwiches, snacks cheeseburgers
Caciocavallo (Kä´-chō-kä-val´-lō) (Italy)	Cows' milk; in Italy, cows' milk or mixtures of sheep's, goats', and cows' milk	3 to 12 months	Piquant, similar to Provolone but not smoked	Firm, lower in milkfat and moisture than Provolone	Light or white interior, clay- or tan-colored surface	Spindle or ten-pin shape, bound with cord, cut pieces	Snacks, sandwiches, cooking, dessert, suitable for grating after prolonged curing

Edam (E´-dăm) (Netherlands)	Partly skimmed cows' milk	2 to 3 months	Mellow, nut-like	Semisoft to firm, smooth, small irregularly shaped or round holes, lower milkfat than Gouda	Creamy yellow or medium-yellow-orange interior, surface coated with red wax	Cannonball-shaped loaf, cut pieces, oblongs	Appetizers, snacks, salads, sandwiches, seafood sauces, dessert
Gouda (Gou´-da) (Netherlands)	Cows' milk, whole or partly skimmed	2 to 6 months	Mellow, nutlike	Semisoft to firm, smooth, small irregularly shaped or round holes, higher milkfat than Edam	Creamy yellow or medium-yellow-orange interior, may or may not have red wax coating	Ball-shaped with flattened top and bottom	Appetizers, snacks, salads, sandwiches, seafood sauces, dessert
Provolone (Prō-vō-lō´-nĕ) also smaller sizes and shapes called Provolette, Provoloncini (Italy)	Cows' milk	2 to 12 months or more	Mellow to sharp, smoky, salty	Firm, smooth	Light creamy interior, light brown or golden yellow surface	Pear-shaped, sausage- and salami-shaped, wedges, slices	Appetizers, sandwiches, snacks, souffle, macaroni and spaghetti dishes, pizza, suitable for grating when fully cured and dried
Swiss, also called Emmentaler (Switzerland)	Cows' milk	3 to 9 months	Sweet, nutlike	Firm, smooth, large round eyes	Light yellow	Segments, pieces, slices	Sandwiches, snacks, sauces, fondue, cheeseburgers

Source: *How to Buy Cheese,* U.S. Department of Agriculture.

Children's clothing sizes

A child's age has little to do with proper clothing size. Weight and height are the best guides.

Size	Height (inches)	Weight (pounds)
	Infants and babies	
3 months	24	13
6 months	26½	18
12 months	29	22
18 months	31½	26
24 months	34	29
36 months	36½	32
	Toddlers	
size 1	31	25
size 2*	34	29
size 3*	37	34
size 4*	40	38
	Children	
size 2*	34	29
size 3*	37	34
size 4*	40	38
size 5	43	44
size 6	46	49
size 6X	48	54
	Girls	
size 7	50	60
size 8	52	67
size 9	54	75
size 10	56	83
size 12	58½	95
size 14	61	107
	Boys	
size 7	48	54
size 8	50	59
size 9	52	65
size 10	54	73
size 11	56	80
size 12	58	87
size 13	59½	93

Size	Height (inches)	Weight (pounds)
size 14	61	100
size 15	62½	107
size 16	64	115
size 17	65	121
size 18	66	126
size 19	67	132
size 20	68	138

*Note that the body measurements for toddlers' sizes 2, 3, and 4 are the same as those for children's sizes 2, 3, and 4.
Source: *Extension Bulletin E-774*, Michigan State University-Coöperative Extension Service.

Children's shoe size growth

Age (years)	Average time between size changes (months)
2–6	1–2
6–10	2–3
10–12	3–4
12–15	4–5
15–20	6

Source: North Dakota State University Extension Service.

Clothing care labels' meanings

When label reads:	It means:
	Machine washable
Machine wash	Wash, bleach, dry, and press by any customary method including commercial laundering and dry cleaning
Home launder only	Same as above but do not use commercial laundering
No chlorine bleach	Do not use chlorine bleach; oxygen bleach may be used
No bleach	Do not use any type of bleach
Cold wash, Cold rinse	Use cold water from tap or cold washing machine setting
Warm wash, Warm rinse	Use warm water or warm washing machine setting
Hot wash	Use hot water or hot washing machine setting
No spin	Remove wash load before final machine spin cycle
Delicate cycle, Gentle cycle	Use appropriate machine setting; otherwise wash by hand
Durable press cycle, Permanent press cycle	Use appropriate machine setting; otherwise use warm wash, cold rinse, and short spin cycle
Wash separately	Wash alone or with like colors
	Non-machine washing
Hand wash	Launder only by hand in lukewarm (hand comfortable) water; may be bleached; may be dry-cleaned
Hand wash only	Same as above, but do not dry-clean
Hand wash separately	Hand wash alone or with like colors
No bleach	Do not use bleach
Damp wipe	Surface clean with damp cloth or sponge
	Home drying
Tumble dry	Dry in tumble dryer at specified setting—high, medium, low, or no heat
Tumble dry, remove promptly	Same as above, but in absence of cool-down cycle remove at once when tumbling stops
Drip dry	Hang wet and allow to dry with hand shaping only
Line dry	Hang damp and allow to dry
No wring, no twist	Hang dry, drip dry, or dry flat only; handle to prevent wrinkles and distortion
Dry flat	Lay garment on flat surface
Block to dry	Maintain original size and shape while drying

	Ironing or pressing
Cool iron	Set iron at lowest setting
Warm iron	Set iron at medium setting
Hot iron	Set iron at hot setting
Do not iron	Do not iron or press with heat
Steam iron	Iron or press with steam
Iron damp	Dampen garment before ironing
	Miscellaneous
Dry-clean only	Garment should be dry-cleaned only, including self-service
Professionally dry-clean only	Do not use self-service dry-cleaning
No dry-clean	Use recommended care instructions; no dry cleaning materials to be used

Source: American Apparel Manufacturers Association.

Concrete estimator

1. Lay out your forms first.

2. Measure the thickness of the concrete to be poured into the forms. Measure at several different points and take an average if the figures vary. Circle the thickness along the top of the chart below.

3. Measure the length and width of the project. Multiply those figures to find the area. Round off to the next-highest 10 square feet.

4. If your area figure is printed on the left-hand side of the chart below, circle it. If not, circle several numbers that, when combined, total your given area. (Example: for 560 square feet, circle 500 plus 50 plus 10.)

5. For thicknesses greater than 5 inches, double a smaller figure. (Example: for 7-inch thickness, double the figure for 3½ inches.)

Cubic yards of concrete required

	Thickness (inches)				
	3	**3½**	**4**	**4½**	**5**
Area (square feet)					
10	0.10	0.11	0.12	0.14	0.16
25	0.23	0.27	0.31	0.35	0.39
50	0.46	0.54	0.62	0.70	0.77
100	0.93	1.08	1.23	1.39	1.54
200	1.85	2.16	2.47	2.78	3.09
300	2.78	3.24	3.70	4.17	4.63
400	3.70	4.32	4.94	5.56	6.17
500	4.63	5.40	6.17	6.94	7.71
600	5.56	6.48	7.41	8.33	9.26
700	6.48	7.56	8.64	9.72	10.80
800	7.40	8.64	9.88	11.11	12.35
900	8.33	9.72	11.11	12.50	13.89
1000	9.26	10.80	12.34	13.89	15.43

Consumer assistance and complaint resources

Subject	Address and Telephone	Type of assistance available
Advertising	Office of the Secretary **Federal Trade Commission** Washington, DC 20580 (202) 523-3598	Individual complaints not handled, but influx from many consumers about same ad will bring investigation of TV, radio, and printed ads.
Aging	Director National Clearinghouse on Aging **Department of Health, Education and Welfare** Washington, DC 20201 (202) 245-2158	State and local agencies handle most administration and information, but complaints and requests for information can also be directed to Washington, DC.
Airlines: **Safety**	Chief Community and Consumer Liaison Division Federal Aviation Administration APA-100 **Department of Transportation** Washington, DC 20591 (202) 426-1960	Nearly every facet of safety, from plane construction to airport operation and even crew health.
Service	Bureau of Consumer Protection **Civil Aeronautics Board** Washington, DC 20428 (202) 673-6047	Fares, routes, service.
Alcoholic beverages	Chief Trade and Consumer Affairs Division Bureau of Alcohol, Tobacco and Firearms **Department of the Treasury** Washington, DC 20226	Content, labeling, taxation, illegal production, advertising of liquor. Issues permits to produce alcohol for industrial or home use, such as gasohol.

Alcoholism	Director National Clearinghouse for Alcohol Information **Department of Health, Education and Welfare** P.O. Box 2345 Rockville, MD 20852 (301) 468-2600	Prevention, control, treatment, information.
Animal health	Information Division Animal and Plant Health Inspection Service **Department of Agriculture** Washington, DC 20250 (202) 447-3977	Quarantine of plants and animals at borders, eradication of pests and diseases of plants and animals. Oversees humane treatment of animals as livestock, pets, circus performers, zoo displays, laboratory subjects, etc.
Animal foods and drugs	Bureau of Veterinary Medicine **Department of Health, Education and Welfare** 5600 Fishers Ln. Rockville, MD 20857 (301) 443-5363	Veterinary preparations, drugs, and equipment, plus pet food labeling.
Antitrust	Assistant Director for Evaluation Bureau of Competition **Federal Trade Commission** Washington, DC 20580 (202) 523-3622	Antitrust violations such as price fixing, monopoly, price discrimination, etc.
Appliances: Service problems	**MACAP** 20 N. Wacker Dr. Chicago, IL 60606 (312) 236-3165	An industry-sponsored arbiter of consumer complaints about faulty major appliances: dehumidifiers, dishwashers, dryers, freezers, garbage disposers, gas incinerators, humidifiers, ranges, refrigerators, room air conditioners, trash compactors, washers, water heaters.

Subject	Address and Telephone	Type of assistance available
Energy efficiency	Office of the Secretary **Federal Trade Commission** Washington, DC 20580 (202) 523-3600	Oversees energy-efficiency labeling of major appliances, furnaces, etc.
Banking		Banks are highly regulated, but by diverse agencies. Complaints and information requests must go to appropriate agency listed and described below. Each agency is interested in interest rates, credit policies, credit cards, business and personal transactions, etc.
Federally chartered	Director Consumer, Community, and Fair Lending Examinations Division Comptroller of the Currency **Department of the Treasury** Washington, DC 20219 (202) 447-1600	These have *national* or *n.a.* in their name.
State chartered (in FRS)	Director Division of Consumer Affairs **Board of Governors of the Federal Reserve System** Washington, DC 20551 (202) 452-3946	Banks chartered by state government must comply with state laws, but also federal laws. State banks in the Federal Reserve System (FRS) are governed by that agency.
State chartered (non-FRS)	Director Office of Consumer Affairs and Civil Rights **Federal Deposit Insurance Corporation** Washington, DC 20429 (202) 389-4427	State banks not in the FRS must follow regulations of the Federal Deposit Insurance Corporation (FDIC).

associations	Consumer Division Office of Community Investment **Federal Home Loan Bank Board** Washington, DC 20552 (202) 377-6237	*association* in their names are regulated by this agency.
Credit unions	Director Division of Consumer Affairs Office of Examination and Insurance **National Credit Union Administration** Washington, DC 20456 (202) 254-8760	Federally chartered credit unions, plus state chartered ones that qualify for deposit insurance, are supervised by this agency.
Business-government relations	Director Office of the Ombudsman **Department of Commerce** Washington, DC 20230 (202) 377-3176	Direct questions and complaints about doing business with U.S. government to this office.
Bus travel	Director Office of Communications and Consumer Affairs **Interstate Commerce Commission** Washington, DC 20423 **800-424-9312** (202) 275-7252 (in Washington, DC)	Rates and service of interstate bus lines.
Chemicals	Office of Toxic Substances (TS-799) **Environmental Protection Agency** Washington, DC 20460 **800-424-9065** (202) 554-1404 (in Washington, D.C.)	Questions about possibly hazardous substances are answered on the spot.

Subject	Address and Telephone	Type of assistance available
Child runaways	**National Runaway Hotline** 800-621-4000 800-972-6004 (in Illinois)	Advice to parents and runaways (confidential).
	Operation Peace of Mind 800-231-6946 800-392-3352 (in Texas) 800-231-6762 (in Alaska, Hawaii)	Funded by State of Texas but offers national referral information on shelter and medical assistance in any state.
Clothing labels	Office of the Secretary **Federal Trade Commission** Washington, DC 20580 (202) 523-3600 (202) 724-1109 (for code names)	Content and care labels must meet federal standards. Manufacturers who identify themselves by a code must list that code with this agency, and they will share it with you. Mislabeling and nonlabeling complaints go here.
Copyright	Information and Publications Section **Copyright Office** 1921 Jefferson Davis Hwy. Arlington, VA (703) 557-8700 (Actual Location)	Information plus assistance (for a fee) in locating copyrights. (For no fee, users can search the card catalog themselves in Arlington, Virginia.)
	Information and Publications Section Library of Congress **Copyright Office** Washington, DC 20559 (Mailing Address)	
Cosmetics	Director Consumer Communications; HFJ-10 Food and Drug Administration/ **Department of Health, Education and Welfare** 5600 Fishers Ln. Rockville, MD 20857	Cosmetics must be honestly and accurately labeled, or you can complain. Also, if you have an unusual reaction to cosmetics possibly mislabeled, harmful, or unclean, report it.

Subject	Contact	Description
Door-to-door sales	Office of the Secretary **Federal Trade Commission** Washington, DC 20580 (202) 523-3598	In short, rules on door-to-door sales are: (1) seller must tell buyers of their right to cancel contract; (2) seller must leave two copies of cancellation form; (3) seller must give a dated receipt or contract with his name and address. This covers *all* selling done in homes, motels, at parties, etc. (except insurance, real estate, securities, and items costing less than $25).
Drugs	Director Consumer Communications; HFJ-10 Food and Drug Administration **Department of Health, Education and Welfare** 5600 Fishers Ln. Rockville, MD 20857 (301) 443-3170	Prescription drugs must be safe, effective, and properly labeled. They also must be advertised in accordance with guidelines. Otherwise, notify this agency. Nonprescription drugs, known as over-the-counter medications, fall under the jurisdiction of the Federal Trade Commission.
Drug abuse	Local DEA offices located in most major cities are listed in telephone directories, or Director Office of Compliance and Regulatory Affairs **Drug Enforcement Administration** Washington, DC 20537 (202) 633-1000	Narcotics and other commonly abused drugs and other substances are watched over by this federal law enforcement agency.
Employment: Discrimination	Director **Equal Employment Opportunity Commission** Washington, DC 20506 (202) 634-6930	Job discrimination based on age, color, national origin, race, religion, or sex in hiring, firing, promotion, or pay, can be investigated and litigated by local offices of this agency or its national headquarters.

Subject	Address and Telephone	Type of assistance available
Safety and health	Director Office of Information Occupational Safety and Health Administration **Department of Labor** Washington, DC 20210 (202) 523-8151	Workers in private industries, plus those in government jobs in states with approved OSHA plans, can file complaints and obtain information here. Workers in transportation-related jobs are covered by the U.S. Department of Transportation, and mines are covered by the Mine Safety and Health Administration of the Department of Labor.
Standards	Director Office of Information and Consumer Affairs Employment Standards Administration **Department of Labor** Washington, DC 20210 (202) 523-8743	Minimum wage, overtime pay, child labor, farm labor, government contracts.
Energy: **General information**	Director Office of Consumer Affairs **Department of Energy** Washington, DC 20585 (202) 252-5141	This agency has nothing to do with rates for energy utilities but is involved with almost all other aspects.
Nuclear regulation	Office of Public Affairs **Nuclear Regulatory Commission** Washington, DC 20555 (202) 492-7715	Safety, security, and antitrust aspects of nuclear power generation.
Solar energy	Director **National Solar Heating and Cooling Information Center** P.O. Box 1607 Rockville, MD 20850 **800-462-4983** **800-523-2929** (in Pennsylvania) **800-523-4700** (in Alaska and Hawaii)	Technical and nontechnical data. This agency does not investigate complaints but will forward appropriate ones to the correct agency.

Environmental protection	Consumer Complaints Public Information Center (PM-215) **Environmental Protection Agency** Washington, DC 20460 (202) 755-0707	Air quality, noise, water, solid waste disposal, toxic substances, pesticides, radiation, etc.
Food: **Meat and poultry**	Meat and Poultry Inspection Food Safety and Quality Service **Department of Agriculture** Washington, DC 20250 (202) 447-3473	Safety, wholesomeness, quality of meat, poultry, and products made from meat or poultry.
Fish	Inspection and Safety Division National Marine Fisheries Service **Department of Commerce** Washington, DC 20235 (202) 634-7458	Quality and safety of fish and fish products.
Other food	Director Consumer Communications, HFJ-10 Food and Drug Administration **Department of Health, Education and Welfare** 5600 Fishers Ln. Rockville, MD 20857 (301) 443-3170	Freedom from harmful additives as well as proper labeling, wholesomeness, quality of nonmeat foods.
Funerals	Office of the Secretary **Federal Trade Commission** Washington, DC 20580 (202) 523-3600	This agency wants funeral directors (1) to give you an itemized bill for all goods and services, (2) to give you a complete list of all available caskets and prices, and (3) to disclose other important information about goods and services.

Subject	Address and Telephone	Type of assistance available
Handicapped:	Chief Clearinghouse on the Handicapped Office for Handicapped Individuals **Department of Health, Education and Welfare** Washington, DC 20201 (202) 245-1961	Information and complaints.
Blind	Director **National Library Service for the Blind and Physically Handicapped** 1291 Taylor St. NW Washington, DC 20542 (202) 882-5500	Talking and braille books or magazines available through regional libraries. If you can't locate a regional participating library, write or call this office.
Travel barriers	Director **Architectural Transportation Barriers Compliance Board** 330 C St. SW Washington, DC 20201 (202) 245-1591	Enforcers of the 1968 Architectural Barriers Act for all federally funded transportation, building, or communications projects.
Health:		
Doctors, dentists, hospitals		State licensing boards and agencies regulate these professions and handle both complaints and specific information.
Medicare		Your local Social Security office is the normal channel for information, your representative the normal channel for complaints.
Medicaid	Director Consumer Affairs Staff Health Care Financing Administration **Department of Health, Education and Welfare** Washington, DC 20201	This federal, state, and local public assistance program is bogged down by at least as much red tape as any bureaucracy. This one office is your major hope for information and complaint assistance.

Mental health	Director National Clearinghouse for Mental Health Information **Department of Health, Education and Welfare** 5600 Fishers Ln. Rockville, MD 20852 (301) 443-4513	Information on parenthood, stress, guilt, learning disabilities, etc.
Hearing aids	Consumer Communications Food and Drug Administration **Department of Health, Education, and Welfare** 5600 Fishers Ln. Rockville, MD 20857 (301) 443-3170	Regulations require hearing aids to be marked—clearly and permanently—with manufacturer's name, model, serial number, year of manufacture, and + symbol to show positive terminal of battery connection. Information and complaints handled by this agency.
Home buying, selling	Director Real Estate Practices Division **Department of Housing and Urban Development** 451 7th St. SW Washington, DC 20410 (202) 755-7038	Private land or home sales.
	Director Office of Interstate Land Sales **Department of Housing and Urban Development** Washington, DC 20410 (202) 755-8182	Buying from developers.

Subject	Address and Telephone	Type of assistance available
Immigration and naturalization	Assistant Commissioner Information Services Division Immigration and Naturalization Service **Department of Justice** 425 Eye St NW Washington, DC 20536 (202) 633-2989	Admission, exclusion, deportation, naturalization of aliens.
Insurance		Most insurance regulation is handled by state agencies, usually a State Commissioner of Insurance. A few provide buyers' guides. Most invite complaints.
Investments: **Business opportunity, franchises, promotions, etc.**	Office of the Secretary **Federal Trade Commission** Washington, DC 20580 (202) 523-3600	Get-rich-quick schemes that don't get you rich quick may be worth complaining about if the promoter failed to disclose risks as well as benefits and misrepresented realistic expectations of profit.
Commodities	Office of Public Information **Commodity Futures Trading Commission** 2033 K St. NW Washington, DC 20581 **800-424-9838** (202) 254-8630 (in Washington, DC) **800-424-9707** (in Alaska and Hawaii)	Commodities that are traded fall into three general areas: farm products such as corn, metals such as gold, and financial papers such as U.S. Treasury bills. Traders and companies that trade these forms of commodities are licensed by this agency, which handles complaints and supplies information.
Stocks and bonds	Director Office of Consumer Affairs **Securities and Exchange Commission** 500 N. Capitol St. NW Washington, DC 20549 (202) 523-3952	The SEC can't protect investors against losses from normal company operations or stock market fluctuations. It does regulate the accuracy of information that major corporations release and does oversee the trading of most stocks and bonds. It provides some general information and investigates most complaints.

	Office of Public Information **New York Stock Exchange** 11 Wall St. New York, NY 10005 (212) 623-3000	Problems with stocks of member firms can be discussed with this agency.
	Office of Public Information **American Stock Exchange** 86 Trinity Pl. New York, NY 10006 (212) 938-6000	Problems with stocks of member firms can be discussed with this agency.
Mail: **Fraud**	Chief Postal Inspector **U.S. Postal Service** Room 3517 Washington, DC 20260 (202) 245-5445	Any illegal, unscrupulous, or misleading schemes that take place through the mails will be investigated and perhaps prosecuted by this policing arm of the U.S. Postal Service. The fastest satisfaction can be had via local postmasters; otherwise, reach this agency
Mail orders and unordered merchandise	Office of the Secretary **Federal Trade Commission** Washington, DC 20580 (202) 523-3600	Unless an offer or ad states otherwise, mail-ordered merchandise must be shipped within thirty days unless you are asked to accept a delay. Otherwise this agency will investigate.
Mail service	Consumer Advocate **U.S. Postal Service** Washington, DC 20260 (202) 245-4514	Complaints about slow or poor mail service.
Unsolicited mail	Consumer Services **Direct Mail Marketing Association** 6 E. 43rd St. New York, NY 10017	A letter to this organization will stop delivery of most ads, catalogs, etc.
	Local Postmaster via Form 2201	To stop delivery of unsolicited pornographic-type mail.
	Local Postmaster via Form 2150	To stop a specific mailer from sending you pornographic-type mail.

Subject	Address and Telephone	Type of assistance available
Maps	National Cartographic Information Center **Geological Survey** 507 National Center Reston, VA 22092 (703) 860-6045	Availability of maps, charts, aerial or satellite photos, and similar cartographic data.
Mobile homes	Office of the Secretary **Federal Trade Commission** Washington, DC 20580 (202) 523-3600	Complaints on sales practices and warranties.
Motor vehicles	Administrator National Highway Traffic Safety Administration **Department of Transportation** Washington, DC 20590 (202) 426-0670	Safety.
	Consumer Affairs Section Antitrust Division **Department of Justice** Washington, DC 20530 (202) 724-6786	Sales practices, warranties.
Movers	Director Consumer Assistance Office **Interstate Commerce Commission** Washington, DC 20423 **800-424-9312** **800-432-4537** (in Florida) (202) 275-0860 (in Washington, DC)	For interstate moves, consumers may request copy of carrier performance report from mover, and mover must provide one. Complaints about rates and performance go to this office. For moves *within* a state, consult a state office.

Subject	Contact	Description
Pensions: **Benefits**	**Pension Benefit Guaranty Corporation** 2020 K St. NW Washington, DC 20006 (202) 254-4817	This agency guarantees that basic retirement benefits will be paid to participants in private pension plans—even if the plan goes out of business. For information or complaints.
Plan information	Director Office of Communications and Public Service Assistance Pension and Welfare Benefit Plans Labor-Management Services Administration **Department of Labor** Washington, DC 20210 (202) 523-8764	Under Employee Retirement Income Security Act (ERISA), pension and welfare fund managers must file annual reports with IRS and give members a copy. Members also must receive a summary of the plan in simple language, as well as a complete plan.
Product safety	Director Office of Communications **Consumer Product Safety Commission** Washington, DC 20207 **800-638-8326** **800-492-8363** (in Maryland) **800-638-8333** (in Puerto Rico, Virgin Islands, Alaska, Hawaii)	Complaints or information about almost anything that might be hazardous: toys, appliances, power equipment, packaging, tools, etc.
Radio: **Amateur**	Amateur Radio Application Office **Federal Communications Commission** Washington, DC 20554 (717) 334-7631	Status of application or information about applying for a license.
Citizens band (CB)	Citizens Band Information Office **Federal Communications Commission** Washington, DC 20554 (717) 334-9167	Information and complaints.

Subject	Address and Telephone	Type of assistance available
Interference complaints	Regional Office of FCC or, in Washington, DC, (301) 436-7590	Information and compliants.
Other information	Chief Consumer Assistance Office **Federal Communications Commission** Washington, DC 20554 (202) 632-7000	Information and complaints.
Rural development	Information Staff Farmers Home Administration **Department of Agriculture** Washington, DC 20250 (202) 447-4323	Information about loan programs: youth project loans, rural housing loans, emergency loans, soil and water conservation loans, etc.
Telephones	Consumer Assistance Office **Federal Communications Commission** Washington, DC 20554 (202) 632-7000	Information and complaints.
Television	Consumer Assistance Office **Federal Communications Commission** Washington, DC 20554 (202) 632-7000	Complaints about programming, information and complaints about licensing.
Trains	**Amtrak** Office of Consumer Relations P.O. Box 2709 Washington, DC 20013 (202) 383-2121	Rate and service information and complaints about Amtrak routes.
	Director Consumer Assistance Office **Interstate Commerce Commission** Washington, DC 20423 **800-424-9312** (202) 275-7806 (in Washington, DC)	Rate and service information and complaints about private lines.

Subject	Agency	Services
	Federal Railroad Administration **Department of Transportation** Washington, DC 20590 (202) 426-0881	
Travel: **Abroad**	Office of Passport Services Bureau of Consular Affairs **Department of State** 1425 K St. NW Washington, DC 20524 (202) 783-8170	Information or complaints, especially about passports, but referrals to other sources of sundry information about overseas travel.
National forests	Director Information Office Forest Service **Department of Agriculture** Washington, DC 20250 (202) 447-3760	Information and complaints.
National parks	Director Office of Public Inquiry National Park Service **Department of the Interior** Washington, DC 20240 (202) 343-7394	Information and complaints.
Volunteers	**ACTION** 806 Connecticut Ave. NW Washington, DC 20525 **800-424-8580** (202) 254-6886 (in Washington, DC)	Information: VISTA (Volunteers in Service to America), RSVP (Retired Senior Volunteer Program), NCSL (National Center for Service-Learning), etc.
Weights and measures	Technical Information and Publications Division **National Bureau of Standards** Washington, DC 20234 (301) 921-3181	Information. Complaints must go to state marketing agencies.

Consumer's calendar of sales and clearances

Although individual stores hold sales at various times during the year, there are traditional times for industrywide sales and clearances.

January
Blankets
Books
Clothes dryers
Craft supplies
Dresses
Freezers
Handbags
Hats
Hobby supplies
Hosiery
Housecoats
Housewares
Lingerie
Linens
Men's coats
Men's haberdashery
Men's shirts
Refrigerators
Shoes
Small appliances
Toiletries
Towels
Toys
Water heaters
Women's sportswear

February
Air conditioners
Auto seat covers
China
Clothes dryers
Curtains
Draperies
Furniture
Glassware
Lawn mowers
Mattresses
Notions
Rugs
Stationery
Used cars

March
Clothes dryers
Insulation
Washing machines

April
Boys' suits
Children's coats
Clothes dryers
Dresses
Insulation
Kitchen cabinets
Men's suits
Millinery
Stoves, ranges
Washing machines

May
Auto tires
Blankets
Cleaning supplies
Housecoats
Linens
Lingerie
Soaps
Television sets
Washing machines

June
Building materials
Dresses
Fabrics
Lumber
Television sets
Washing machines

July
Children's clothes
Freezers
Fuel oil
Handbags
Hats
Hosiery
Housecoats
Lingerie
Men's haberdashery
Men's shirts
Refrigerators
Shoes
Toiletries

August
Air conditioners
Blankets
Boys' suits
Carpets
Children's coats
Curtains
Draperies
Furniture
Fur coats
Linens
Men's coats
Men's suits
Tires (auto)
Towels
Used cars
Women's coats

September
Auto batteries
Auto mufflers
China
Fabrics
Glassware
Hardware
Housewares
New cars

October
None

November
Auto seat covers
Children's coats
Fabrics
Snowblowers
Stoves, ranges
Used cars
Water heaters
Women's coats

December
Boys' suits
Children's clothes
Children's coats
Men's suits
Used cars

Cooking ingredient equivalents

Food	Quantity	Yield
Apples	1 medium	1 cup sliced
Barley, regular	1 cup uncooked	4 cups cooked
Barley, quick	1 cup uncooked	3 cups cooked
Bread crumbs	3 to 4 slices bread	1 cup dry crumbs
	1 slice bread	¾ cup soft crumbs
Cabbage	1 pound	4 cups shredded
Cheese	¼ pound	1 cup shredded
Graham crackers	15	1 cup fine crumbs
Soda crackers	16	1 cup coarse crumbs
	22	1 cup fine crumbs
Cornmeal	1 cup uncooked	4 cups cooked mush
Hominy grits	1 cup uncooked	4 cups cooked
Dry beans	1 cup	2½ cups cooked
All-purpose flour	1 pound	4 cups sifted
Macaroni and spaghetti	½ pound uncooked (2 cups)	4 cups cooked
Noodles	½ pound uncooked (4 cups)	4 cups cooked
Onion	1 medium	½ cup chopped
Rice	1 cup	3½ cups cooked
Quick or old-fashioned oats	2 cups	4 cups oatmeal
Shortening	1 pound	2 cups
Brown sugar	1 pound	2¼ cups firmly packed
Confectioner's sugar	1 pound	3½ cups sifted
Granulated sugar	1 pound	2¼ cups
Regular butter or magarine	1 pound	4 sticks 2 cups
Whipped butter or margarine	1 pound	6 sticks 2 8-ounce containers 3 cups

Source: The Quaker Oats Company.

Cooking measurements substitutions

Units	Teaspoonfuls	Tablespoon-fuls	Fluid ounces	Cupfuls	Liquid pints	Liquid quarts	Milliliters	Liters
1 teaspoonful equals	1	1/3	1/6				5	
1 tablespoonful equals	3	1	1/2	1/16	1/32		15	
1 fluid ounce equals	6	2	1	1/8	1/16	1/32	30	
1 cupful equals	48	16	8	1	1/2	1/4	240	0.24
1 liquid pint equals			16	2	1	1/2	470	0.47
1 liquid quart equals			32	4	2	1	950	0.95
1 milliliter equals	1/5						1	1/1000
1 liter equals			34	4.2	2.1	1.06	1000	1

Source: *Special Publication 430*, National Bureau of Standards.

Cooking times and yields for fresh vegetables

Vegetable	Cooking time after water returns to boil (Minutes)	Approximate purchase for six servings (about ½ cup each) (Pounds)
Asparagus	10–20 (whole spears)	2½ (for spears)
	5–15 (cuts and tips)	1¾–2 (for cuts and tips)
Beans, lima	25–30	2¾ (in pods)
Beans, snap	12–16 (1-inch pieces)	1
Beets	30–45 (young, whole)	2½ (with tops) or 1½ (without tops)
	45–90 (older, whole)	
	15–25 (sliced or diced)	
Broccoli	10–15 (heavy stalks, split)	1¾
Brussels sprouts	15–20	1¼
Cabbage	3–10 (shredded)	1¼
	10–15 (wedges)	1½
Carrots	15–20 (young, whole)	1½ (without tops)
	20–30 (older, whole)	
	10–20 (sliced or diced)	
Cauliflower	8–15 (separated)	2
	15–25 (whole)	
Celery	15–18 (cut up)	1½
Corn	5–15 (on cob)	3 (in husks)
Kale	10–15	1¼ (untrimmed)
Okra	10–15	1¼
Onions, mature	15–30	1¾
Parsnips	20–40 (whole)	1½
	8–15 (quartered)	
Peas	12–16	3 (in pods)
Potatoes	25–40 (whole, medium)	1½
	20–25 (quartered)	
	10–15 (diced)	
Spinach	3–10	2 (untrimmed) or 1½ (prepackaged)
Squash, summer	8–15 (sliced)	1½
Squash, winter	15–20 (cut up)	3
Sweet potatoes	35–55 (whole)	1½
Tomatoes	7–15 (cut up)	1¼
Turnip greens	10–30	2¾ (untrimmed)
Turnips	20–30 (whole)	1¾ (without tops)
	10–20 (cut up)	

Source: *Vegetables in Family Meals,* U.S. Department of Agriculture.

Dinnerware item sizes and uses

"Trade sizes" for plates, bowls, and similar dinnerware items are measured from the inside shoulder on one side to the outer edge of the other side. Actual size is from outer rim to outer rim, the true diameter.

Item	Trade size (inches)	Actual size (inches)	Suggestions for use
	Plates		
Service or place	10½–11	11½–12	On table between courses.
Dinner	9½–10	10½–11	Main course.
Luncheon or breakfast	8½–9	9½–10	Also for buffet.
Salad	7½–8	8½–9	Salads, fish courses, dessert, tea, with sherbet glass, or under lug soup.
Pie	6½–7	7½–8	Dessert or salad. Size determines other uses.
Bread and butter	4½–5	5½–6	Also for relishes. Not adequate as dessert plate.
Coaster	3–3½	3½–4	For glass, butter pat, or as ashtray.
	Deeper Dishes		
Fruit	4½–5	5½–6	At breakfast for fruit, for individual vegetable servings.
Cereal	5½–6	6–7	Cereal, green salad, soup, dessert (baked apple, etc.). Place on salad plate to serve.
	Soups		
Plate, coupe	7½–8	8–9	Often used for cold cereals too.
Rim soup	7½–8	8–9	Serve on place plate.
Cream soup	7½–8	8–9	Two-handled cup (more formal) is served with own saucer.
Lug soup	5½–6	6–7	Soup, cereal, tossed salad, or dessert.
Covered soup	5½–6	6–7	Onion soup or marmite. If ovenproof, used as casserole.
	Vegetables		
Nappie (round)	Varies to 9	Varies to 10	Vegetables, fruit desserts.
Baker (oval)			Vegetables only.

Covered nappie	Varies to 12	Varies to 12	For keeping vegetables warm.
Covered casserole			Usually ovenproof; otherwise used like covered nappie.
Salad bowl			Usually deeper and larger.
	Platters		
Oval, small	8–10	10–11	Breakfast platter. Also for asparagus or corn instead of deeper vegetable dishes.
Oval, medium	10–12	12–15	Luncheon size, for chops, chicken, or small steaks.
Oval, large	12–15	14–17	Roasts, large steaks, turkey.
Chop	Varies to 15	Varies to 15	Meats, sandwiches, iced layer cake, hors d'oeuvres.
Pickle	7½–8	7½–8	Oval dish for relishes; also used under sauce boat.
	Sauce Boats		
Fast stand			For gravy, mayonnaise, hollandaise, etc. Has drip stand on foot.
Regular			Use on pickle dish; other uses as above.
Sugar and cream			As indicated by name.
	Cups and Saucers		
Tea			Used for many things—from bouillon to coffee.
Coffee			For breakfast.
Demitasse or afterdinner			Small cup usually used for black coffee. Served away from table.

Source: *China, Glass, and Decorative Accessories.*

Dinnerware sets: contents of

16-Piece Set
4 breakfast plates
4 bread and butters
4 cups and saucers

20-Piece Set
4 breakfast plates
4 bread and butters
4 cups and saucers
4 fruits

23-Piece Set
4 breakfast plates
4 bread and butters
4 cups and saucers
4 fruits
1 sugar and cover
1 creamer

35-Piece Set
6 breakfast plates
6 bread and butters
6 cups and saucers
6 fruits
1 sugar and cover
1 creamer
1 small nappie
1 small platter

53-Piece Set
8 dinner plates
8 bread and butters
8 fruits
8 soups
8 cups and saucers
1 sugar and cover
1 creamer
1 medium nappie or baker
1 medium platter

63-Piece Set
Same as 53, plus:
8 salad plates
1 large platter
1 additional nappie or baker

94-Piece Set
12 dinner plates
12 bread and butters
12 salads
12 soups
12 fruits
12 cups and saucers
1 sugar and cover
1 creamer
1 medium platter
1 large platter
1 baker
1 covered nappie
1 gravy
1 pickle

Source: *China, Glass and Decorative Accessories.*

Drapery rod length guide

For draperies to open ("stack back") beyond the window frame opening, so that the entire glass window can be uncovered, you need to know how far on each side of the window to extend the drapery rod. The following chart shows both the width to allow on each side for stack-back and the entire length of the drapery rod you need.

If the glass is (inches)	The stack-back* should be (inches)	Your rod length and finished drapery width should be (Add for overlaps and returns) (inches)
38	26	64
44	28	72
50	30	80
56	32	88
62	34	96
68	36	104
75	37	112
81	39	120
87	41	128
94	42	136
100	44	144
106	46	152
112	48	160
119	49	168
125	51	176
131	53	184
137	55	192
144	56	200
150	58	208
156	60	216
162	62	224
169	63	232
175	65	240
181	67	248
187	69	256

Note: Figures are based on average pleating and medium-weight fabric.
For extra-bulky fabrics, add to stack-back to compensate for the additional space they require.
*For one-way draws, deduct 7 inches from stack-back.
Source: Kirsch Company.

Eggs: cost per pound

To get the most egg for the money, you have to compare the prices of the various sizes. Eggs are sold by weight, a fact known by few people. Extra-large eggs weigh 27 ounces per dozen, large 24, medium 21, and small 18. Using this chart, you can convert price per dozen of the various sizes into price per pound.

Price per dozen (by size)				Price per pound
Extra-large	Large	Medium	Small	¢/Lb.
.32	.28	.24	.21	.19
.33½	.30	.26	.23	.20
.36	.32	.28	.24	.21
.38	.34	.29½	.25½	.22½
.41	.36	.32	.27	.24
.42	.38	.33	.28	.25
.46	.40	.35	.30	.27
.47	.42	.37	.32	.28
.49	.44	.38	.33	.29
.52	.46	.41	.35	.31
.54	.48	.42	.36	.32
.56	.50	.43	.37	.33
.59	.52	.46	.39	.35
.61	.54	.47	.41	.36
.62	.56	.49	.42	.37
.65	.58	.50½	.43½	.38½
.68	.60	.53	.45	.40
.69	.62	.54	.46	.41
.72	.64	.55½	.47½	.42½
.74	.66	.58	.50	.44
.76	.68	.59	.51	.45
.78½	.70	.61	.52½	.46½
.81	.72	.63	.54	.48
.83	.74	.64	.56	.49
.85	.76	.66	.59	.50½
.88	.80	.69	.60	.52
.90	.82	.72	.63	.53½
.93	.84	.73	.64	.56

Price per dozen (by size)				Price per pound
Extra-Large	Large	Medium	Small	¢/Lb
.97	.86	.75	.65	.57½
1.00	:89	.77	.66	.59
1.02	.91	.79	.68	.60½
1.05	.93	.81	.70	.62
1.07	.95	.83	.71	.63½
1.10	.98	.85	.73	.65
1.12	1.00	.87	.75	.66½
1.15	1.02	.89	.77	.68
1.17	1.04	.91	.78	.69½
1.20	1.07	.93	.80	.71
1.22	1.09	.95	.82	.72½
1.25	1.11	.97	.83	.74
1.27	1.13	.99	.85	.75½
1.30	1.16	1.01	.87	.77
1.32	1.18	1.03	.88	.78½
1.35	1.20	1.05	.90	.80
1.38	1.22	1.07	.92	.81½
1.40	1.25	1.09	.93	.83
1.43	1.27	1.11	.95	.84½
1.45	1.29	1.13	.97	.86
1.48	1.31	1.15	.98	.87½
1.50	1.34	1.17	1.00	.89
1.53	1.36	1.19	1.02	.90½
1.55	1.38	1.21	1.04	.92
1.58	1.40	1.23	1.05	.93½
1.60	1.43	1.25	1.07	.95
1.63	1.45	1.27	1.09	.96½
1.65	1.47	1.29	1.10	.98
1.68	1.49	1.31	1.12	.99½

Electrical appliance cost of operation

Costs are figured at 10¢ per kwh (kilowatt hour) for your convenience. If local rates are now 6¢ per kwh, simply multiply the costs in this chart by .6. (Example: Clothes dryer–electric shows $2.60 for 10¢ per kwh. For 6¢ per kwh, $2.60 × .6 = $1.56.)

Appliance	Wattage rating (or other information)	Average hours used per month	Average kwh per month	Cost (per month) at 10¢ per kwh
Air conditioner (central unit)	24,000–60,000 BTU	3,000–8,000 kwh (per season)		$300–800 (for season)
Air conditioner (window unit)	5,000–30,000 BTU	1,000–3,000 kwh (per season)		$100–300 (for season)
Bake oven	800–1,000	10	10	1.00
Barbecuer (outdoor)	20	25	less than 1	.10
Blanket, electric	100–200	240	24–48	2.40– 4.80
Blender, food	200–300	2	less than 1	.10
Blender, drink	200–300	2	less than 1	.10
Bottle sterilizer	450	45	20	2.00
Bottle warmer	100–500	20	2–10	.20– 1.00
Broiler, rotisserie	1,500	10	15	1.50

Can opener	175	1	less than 1	.10
Casserole	1,300	20	26	2.60
Chafing dish/Fondue	800	3	2	.20
Cleaner, vacuum	300–1,000	15	4–10	.40– 1.00
Clipper, hair	10–20	4	less than 1	.10
Clock	3–7	720	2–5	.20– .50
Coffee maker	400–1,000	15	6	.60
Coffee maker (instant brew)	1,200–1,500	4	5	.50
Coffee percolator	300–500	15	5	.50
Clothes dryer—electric heating elements	4,500–9,000	20–10	90	9.00
Clothes dryer—gas-heated, electric control	200	20	4	.40
Corn popper	450–1,300	2	1	.10
Deep-fat fryer	1,000–1,350	10	10–15	1.00– 1.50
Defroster refrigerator	300–500	1	less than 1	.10
Dehumidifier	300–650	360 (12 hrs. day in summer)	100–225	10–22.50
Dishwasher with heating element	1,000–1,600	30	30–45	3– 4.50
Dishwasher without heating element	250	30	75	.75
Door chime	15	2	less than 1	.10
Dryer, hair (blower)	200–1,200	10	8	.80
Egg cooker	500	10	5	.50
Electrocutor (insect)	5–250	100	1	.10
Electronic filter (central system)	11–60	100	5	.50
Electronic filter (console model)	175–225	100	20	2.00

Appliance	Wattage rating (or other information)	Average hours used per month	Average kwh per month	Cost (per month) at 10¢ per kwh
Fan, attic	300–500	100	40	4.00
Fan, portable	50–100	100	10	1.00
Floor washer	425	2	1	.10
Floor waxer-polisher	400	5	2	.20
Food grinder	500	4	2	.20
Foot warmer	50–100	10	1	.10
Freezer, food storage	250–650	150	50–100	5.00–10.00
Fry pan, skillet	1,100–1,250	15	16	1.60
Fry pan, multicooker	1,150–1,250	20	23	2.30
Furnace, oil—electric controls	300	300 kwh. per season		30.00
Furnace, gas—electric controls	25	10 kwh. per season		1.00
Furnace blower	350–600	180	54–108	5.40–10.80
Garbage disposal	350–650	3	1–2	.10– .20
Griddle, automatic	1,450	10	14	1.40
Grill	660–1,100	5	3	.30
Grinder, meat	100	5	less than 1	.10
Heat lamp (infrared)	125–250	10	2	.20
Heat pump		(.63–.88 per sq.ft. for season)		
Heater, radiant	1,000	15	15	1.50
Heating, electric resistance	With proper insulation; $1.00–$1.20 per sq.ft. for heating season			
Heating pad	60–100	10	1	.10
Hot dog cooker	1,500	6	9	.90
Hot plate	1,000	15	15	1.50
Humidifier	500	20	15	1.50

Ice cream freezer	100–500	2	less than 1	.10
Ice crusher	100	10	1	.10
Incinerator	600	16	10	1.00
Iron, hand, dry	1,100	10	11	1.10
Iron, hand, steam	1,100	10	11	1.10
Iron, hand, steam and spray	1,100	10	11	1.10
Ironer	1,500	10	15	1.50
Juicer	100	3	less than 1	.10
Kitchen ventilating fan	30–100	15	less than 1	.10
Knife, carving	100	6	less than 1	.10
Knife sharpener	50–100	2	less than 1	.10
Light (night)	1	300	less than 1	.10
Lighter, charcoal	500–1,000	2	1–2	.10– .20
Lighting	25–300	150	75–150	4.50–15.00
Lighting, post	100	300	30	3.00
Log, electric	40–1,000	30	5–30	.05– 3.00
Mechanical exerciser	500	30	15	1.50
Mixer, food	100–350	6	less than 1	.10
Organ, electric	40–100	30	less than 1	.10
Oven, microwave	90–650	20	10	1.00
Oven, toaster and broiler	800	10	8	.80
Pressure cooker	1,400	10	13	1.30
Projector, movie	500	4	2	.20
Projector, slide	500	2	1	.10

Appliance	Wattage rating (or other information)	Average hours used per month	Average kwh per month	Cost (per month) at 10¢ per kwh
Radio	60–350	60	3–20	.30– 2.00
Range hood	60–150	10	1	.10
Range, electric	8,000–23,000	All meals	150	15.00
Range, table	1,000–1,300	10	12	1.20
Record player	50–100	10	1	.10
Record player, hi-fi and stereo sound	50–100	10	1	.10
Refrigerator, conventional	200–500	180	36–90	3.60– 9.00
Refrigerator, ice maker	500–750	180	165–210	16.50–21.00
Refrigerator, combination (freezer)	500–750	180	90–135	9– 3.50
Rotisserie	1,200–1,400	4	5	.50
Roaster	1,300–1,600	30	40	4.00
Sandwich grill	650–1,100	10	10	1.00
Saucepan	700–1,200	30	20–35	2.00– 3.50
Sewing machine	75–100	10	1	.10
Shaver	10–15	8	less than 1	.10
Slicer, meat	100	1	less than 1	.10
Slow cooker	70–200	60	12	1.20
Sunlamp	250–500	5	2	.30
Tea kettle	550–1,500	15	8–20	.80– 2.00
Tea pot	400	5	2	.20
Television (black and white)	150–400	200	60	6.00
Television (color)	300–450	200	80	8.00
Toaster, automatic	1,200	5	6	.60
Trash compactor	300–500	4	2	.20

Vacuum cleaner	350–750	6	2–5	.20– .50
Vaporizer	350–850	5	4	.40
Vibrator (hand type)	50	10	less than 1	.10
Vibrator (in chair)	50	40	2	.20
Vibrator (in mattress)	10	100	1	.10
Vibrator (foot massager)	50	40	2	.20
Waffle iron	1,200	5	6	.60
Warming tray	100–150	6	1	.10
Washer, automatic	500–1,000	25	10–25	1.00– 2.50
Washer, nonautomatic	350	15	5	.50
Waste disposer	500–750	4	2	.20
Water heater, automatic	Normally 5,000	Automatic 400 (Family of 4)		40.00
Water pump, shallow well (home)	500	30	15	1.50
Water pump, deep well (entire farmstead)	500–1,500	60	30–90	3.00– 9.00
Window ventilator	600–1,000	60	36–60	3.60– 6.00

Source: *Cost of Operation of Electrical Equipment*. Kansas State University Extension, 1978.

Electrical wiring box capacities

Boxes for household wiring are rated by the National Electrical Code for the maximum number of wires and pieces of hardware they can hold safely. The larger the volume (in cubic inches) of the box, the more it can hold. When in doubt, always use a larger box than the code requires; it's safer as well as practical. To use this chart, follow this procedure:

1. Count the number of hot and neutral wires entering or leaving the box.
2. Add one for grounding wires.
3. Add one if you use cable clamps built into the box. (External clamps do not have to be counted.)
4. Add one if you are going to connect a lamp or other device directly to the box.
5. For lamp installations, if a threaded rod or similar support takes up space inside the box, add one unless you added one in step 3 above; if so, disregard this step.

Box type and dimensions (in approximate inches)	Cubic-inch capacity (approximate)	Maximum number of conductors plus hardware #14 wire	#12 wire
Octagon			
3¼ (1½ deep)	11	5	4
3½ (1½ deep)	12	5	5
4 (1½ deep)	17	8	7
4 (2 deep)	24	11	10
Square			
4 (1½ deep)	23	11	10
4 (2 deep)	32	15	14
4-11/16 (1½ deep)	32	16	14
Switch box			
3 x 2 x 1½	8	3	3
3 x 2 x 2	11	5	4
3 x 2 x 2¼	11	5	5
3 x 2 x 2½	13	6	5
3 x 2 x 2¾	15	7	6
3 x 2 x 3½	18	9	8
4 x 2⅛ x 1½	11	5	4
4 x 2⅛ x 1⅞	14	6	6
4 x 2⅛ x 2⅛	16	7	6

Source: *How to Improve Damn Near Everything Around Your Home,* Peterson and Kesselman-Turkel.

Energy conservation from common home improvements

Percent reduction in energy consumption	Home improvement
2.3	Switching to high-performance air conditioner
2.6	Setting back temperature from 72° F. to 68° F. between 8:00 P.M. and 8:00 A.M.
3.8	Adding flue damper
4.6	Switching to high-performance furnace
1.1	Changing from metal to wood casement windows
3.8	Adding storm doors
5.0	Adding storm door plus vestibule on north door
5.0	Increasing wall insulation by 12 percent
2.7	Insulating exposed basement wall
5.0	Reducing window area by 25 percent
7.2	Adding storm windows
8.0	Reducing use of electric lights and appliances by 25 percent

Source: *Residential Energy Conservation,* U.S. Department of Housing and Urban Development

Energy use for your own home: an audit

Step 1: Enter your heating energy use. If the energy source you heat with is used for nothing but heating your home, you can skip points A and C. Just enter your use in the table under point B in this step. If that is not the case, you need to do a few more calculations. However, this is pretty simple. Since you want only the amount of energy used for heating your home, you need to figure out how much energy you used for nonheating purposes such as cooking or water heating. The way you can do that is to use an average of two months of bills when your energy use didn't include home heating. Obviously, one good choice would be May and June.

HERE'S HOW IT WORKS:

A. Add the amount of fuel you used for May and June and divide by two. This will be the average monthly nonheating use.

Average monthly nonheating use = ___________

B. Now enter your fuel use for October through April for the last winter. Note the units of measurement. (Kwh for electricity, CCF or therms for natural gas, gallons for oil or LP gas). You'll need these units in step 2.

Type of energy ____________
Use units ________________

MONTH	
October	
November	
December	
January	
February	
March	
April	
TOTAL	

C. Finally, multiply the average nonheating use by the number of winter months (seven) and subtract this product from the total you got in point B. The answer is your total winter heating energy use.

Total energy use (from B)	________
– (7 × Nonheating energy use (from A))	________
= TOTAL HEATING ENERGY USE	________

Step 2: Convert your use to BTUs. Enter your heating use from point B or C above in the appropriate blank for the kind of energy you use to heat. Then multiply it by the number given. This converts your energy use to BTUs.

Electricity	________	Kwh × 3,413 =	________	BTU
Natural gas	________	CCF × 100,000 =	________	BTU
Fuel oil	________	Gal. × 140,000 =	________	BTU
LP Gas	________	Gal. × 95,000 =	________	BTU

Step 3: Find the degree days. Consult you local library or power company to find the number of degree days for the last heating season.

Season degree days ________

Step 4: Calculate your energy index. You can use this index number to compare your house to other houses and to itself over time.

HERE'S HOW:

A. First divide the BTU total (step 2) by the degree days (step 3). This gives your energy consumption corrected for temperature.

B. Then divide the result of point A above by the square feet of the heated areas of your house. The result is your Heating Energy Index.

A. _____ BTU ÷ _____ Degree Days = _____ BTU/D.D.

B. _____ BTU/D.D. ÷ _____ Ft^2 = _____ BTU/D.D.Ft^2 *(Energy Index)*

With your energy index, locate your house on the energy thermometer below:

EXCELLENT	GOOD	FAIR	POOR
0–6	7–9	10–12	13 +

Source: University of Wisconsin Extension.

Fabric ironing guide

Dry or steam	Temperature setting	Fabric to be ironed	Ironing instructions
Dry	Cool	Acetates	Iron fabric on wrong side to prevent shine. Do not dampen, or water spotting may occur.
Dry	Cool	Acrylics (Acrilan, Creslan, Orlon, Zefran)	Iron fabric blends with setting at lowest temperature of two fabrics. Follow label directions for garment care.
Dry	Permanent press	Metallics	Press on wrong side.
	Permanent press	Patent leather	Use brown paper as a pressing cloth. Press on wrong side.
Dry	Permanent press	Suede leather	Cover ironing board with brown paper to prevent suede from rubbing off. Press on wrong side.
Dry	Permanent press	Silk	Iron on wrong side. (Some silk can be steam ironed; consult label on garment.)
Dry	Permanent press	Permanent press touch-ups	Dry iron lightweight durable press 100-percent synthetics. If necessary, remove remaining wrinkles with steam. Use press cloth to avoid shine.
Dry	Permanent press	Polyesters (Dacron, Fortrel, Kodel)	Polyester fabrics launder and dry quickly. A light touch-up may be desirable for resetting pleats, etc.
Steam and spray or dry	Permanent press	Permanent press blends of cotton and polyesters	To help restore creases or pleats, test inconspicuous area. If shine or color change occurs, use press cloth. Iron dry or with steam and permanent press spray.
Steam or spray	Permanent press	Wash-and-wear cotton, rayons, nylons, triacetates (Arnel)	Steam and/or spray.

Steam or dry	Wool	Woolens	Steam press on wrong side. Use thin, dry pressing cloth to prevent shine or hard-finished worsted or when using a dry iron.
Dry or steam and spray	Cotton	Cottons, starched clothes, sheer linen	Iron dark colors on wrong side to prevent shine. Iron embroidery and lacquered prints on wrong side to prevent damage. Heavy fabrics should be dampened.
Dry or steam and spray	Linen	Linen	Predampen for best results. Iron table linens on right side to bring up sheen, dark linen on wrong side to prevent shine.

Source: General Electric Housewares Division.

Fiber trademarks compared to generic names

Trademark	Generic name	Manufacturer
Acrilan	acrylic, modacrylic	Monsanto Textiles Company
Anso	nylon	Allied Chemical Corp., Fibers Div.
Antron	nylon	E.I. du Pont de Nemours & Co., Inc.
Ariloft	acetate	Eastman Kodak Company, Tennessee Eastman Co. Division
Arnel	triacetate	Celanese Fibers Marketing Co. Celanese Corp.
Avlin	polyester	Avtex Fibers Inc.
Avril	rayon (high wet)	Avtex Fibers Inc.
Beau-Grip	rayon	Beaunit Corporation
Beaunit Nylon	nylon	Beaunit Corporation
Bi-Loft	acrylic	Monsanto Textiles Company
Blue "C"	nylon, polyester	Monsanto Textiles Company
Cadon	nylon	Monsanto Textiles Company
Cantrece	nylon	E.I. du Pont de Nemours & Co., Inc.
Caprolan	nylon, polyester	Allied Chemical Corp., Fibers Div.
Celanese	nylon, acetate	Celanese Fibers Marketing Co., Celanese Corp.
Chromspun	acetate	Eastman Kodak Company, Tennessee Eastman Co. Division
Coloray	rayon	Courtaulds North America Inc.
Cordura	nylon	E.I. du Pont de Nemours & Co., Inc.
Courtaulds Nylon	nylon	Courtaulds North America Inc.
Crepeset	nylon	American Enka Company
Creslan	acrylic	American Cyanamid Company
Cumuloft	nylon	Monsanto Textiles Company
Dacron	polyester	E.I. du Pont de Nemours & Co., Inc.
Elura	modacrylic	Monsanto Textiles Company
Encron	polyester	American Enka Company
Enkaloft	nylon	American Enka Company
Enkalure	nylon	American Enka Company
Enkasheer	nylon	American Enka Company
Enkrome	rayon	American Enka Company
Estron	acetate	Eastman Kodak Company, Tennessee Eastman Co. Division
Fibro	rayon	Courtaulds North America Inc.
Fina	acrylic	Monsanto Textiles Company
Fortrel	polyester	Fiber Industries Inc., Marketed by Celanese Fibers Marketing Co., a Division of Celanese Corp.

Trademark	Generic name	Manufacturer
Herculon	olefin	Hercules Inc., Fibers Division
Hollofil	polyester	E.I. du Pont de Nemours & Co., Inc.
Kevlar	aramid	E.I. du Pont de Nemours & Co., Inc.
Kodel	polyester	Eastman Kodak Company, Tennessee Eastman Co. Division
Lanese	acetate, polyester	Celanese Fibers Marketing Co. Celanese Corp.
Loftura	acetate	Eastman Kodak Company, Tennessee Eastman Co. Division
Lurex	metallic	Dow Badische Company
Lycra	spandex	E.I. du Pont de Nemours & Co., Inc.
Marvess	olefin	Phillips Fibers Corp., Subsidiary of Phillips Petroleum Co.
Monvelle	biconstituent nylon/spandex	Monsanto Textiles Company
Multisheer	nylon	American Enka Company
Nomex	aramid	E.I. du Pont de Nemours & Co., Inc.
Orlon	acrylic	E.I. du Pont de Nemours & Co., Inc.
Polyloom	olefin	Chevron Chemical Co., Fibers Div.
Qiana	nylon	E.I. du Pont de Nemours & Co., Inc.
Quintess	polyester	Phillips Fibers Corp., Subsidiary of Phillips Petroleum Co.
SEF	modacrylic	Monsanto Textiles Company
Shantura	polyester	Rohm and Haas Co., Fibers Div.
Shareen	nylon	Courtaulds North America Inc.
Spectran	polyester	Monsanto Textiles Company
Strialine	polyester	American Enka Company
Teflon	fluorocarbon	E.I. du Pont de Nemours & Co., Inc.
Textura	polyester	Rohm and Haas Co., Fibers Div.
Trevira	polyester	Hoechst Fibers Industries
Twisloc	polyester	Monsanto Textiles Company
Ulstron	nylon	Monsanto Textiles Company
Ultron	nylon	Monsanto Textiles Company
Vecana	nylon	Chevron Chemical Company
Vectra	olefin	Vectra Corp., Subsidiary of Chevron Chemical Company
Verel	modacrylic	Eastman Kodak Company, Tennessee Eastman Co. Division
Vycron	polyester	Beaunit Corporation
Xena	rayon (high wet)	Beaunit Corporation
X-Static	nylon, metallic	Rohm and Haas Co., Fibers Div.
Zantrel	rayon (high wet)	American Enka Company
Zeflon	nylon	Dow Badische Company
Zefran	acrylic, nylon, polyester	Dow Badische Company

Source: Man-Made Fiber Producers Association.

Fiber characteristics (synthetic)

	Acetate	Acrylic	Aramid	Metallic	Modacrylic	Nylon	Olefin	Polyester	Rayon	Saran	Spandex	Triacetate	Vinyon
Absorbent									●				
Colorfast		●		●		●	●	●	●	●		●	
Easy to dye	●		●			●			●			●	
Easy to launder		●	●	●		●	●	●	●		●	●	
Easy to iron			●			●		●	●			●	
Elastic						●					●		
Exceptional durability			●	●		●	●	●		●			
Flame resistant			●		●					●			
Good drapability	●		●			●			●			●	
Good shape retention		●			●	●		●			●	●	
Quick drying		●	●		●	●	●	●			●	●	
Resilient		●	●		●	●		●					
Resistant to:													
abrasion			●			●	●	●					
chemicals		●	●		●	●	●	●		●			
moth	●	●	●	●	●	●	●	●	●	●	●	●	●
mildew	●	●	●	●	●	●	●	●		●	●	●	●
oil and grease		●	●			●					●		
pilling	●								●			●	
stretching			●					●					
soil			●				●						
shrinking		●	●	●		●		●		●		●	
weather		●		●	●		●	●	●	●			
Soft	●	●			●				●				
Strong			●			●	●	●		●			
Warm		●			●	●		●					
Wide color range	●	●			●	●		●	●			●	
Wrinkle resistant		●						●			●	●	

Source: Man-Made Fiber Producers Association, Inc.

Firewood heating values and weights

Not all types of wood give the same amount of heat per cord. This chart can help you pick the best value in wood for your dollar. Also, wet (green) wood provides less heat than dried wood, and greenness can be gauged by weight, also figured into this chart. The BTU, British Thermal Unit, is a standard unit of heat measurement that is useful for comparing various materials such as firewood. A *cord* of wood is a pile 4 feet high, 8 feet long, and 4 feet wide. A *face cord* is a pile 4 feet high and 8 feet long but as wide as the seller chooses to make it. Thus, you can buy a 16-inch face cord (which is 16 inches thick), a 24-inch face cord (24 inches thick), and so forth. We use the full cord here.

	Weight of one cord (pounds)		Available heat (Millions of BTUs)	
Species	**Green**	**Air-dried**	**Green**	**Air-dried**
Ash	3,840	3,440	16.5	20.0
Aspen	3,440	2,160	10.3	12.5
Beech	4,320	3,760	17.3	21.8
Paper Birch	3,800	3,040	16.7	18.2
Yellow Birch	4,560	3,680	17.3	21.3
Elm	4,320	2,900	14.3	17.2
Hickory	5,040	4,240	20.7	24.6
Soft Maple	4,000	3,200	15.0	18.6
Hard Maple	4,480	3,680	18.4	21.3
Red Oak	5,120	3,680	17.9	21.3
White Oak	5,040	3,920	19.2	22.7
White Pine	2,880	2,080	12.1	13.3

Source: University of Wisconsin Extension.

Firewood moisture content compared to heat value

Moisture content of firewood helps determine how much heat you get from it. For most purposes, fully air-dried wood is the most efficient. Greener wood wastes more heat because your fire first must dry out the wood and then burn it.

Condition of wood	Relative heat value (percent of heat compared to fully air-dried wood)	Percent of log that is moisture
Green in fall, winter, spring	85	80
Green in summer	93	65
Wood air-dried for 3 months	97	35
Wood air-dried for 6 months	98	30
Wood air-dried for 12 months	100	25

Source: *Heating with Wood,* U.S. Department of Energy.

Floor tile estimator

The table below shows the number of 9-x-9-inch floor tiles required for rooms of various sizes. A 5-percent allowance for cutting and waste has been figured into these calculations.

Length (feet)	Width (feet)														
	4	5	6	7	8	9	10	11	12	13	14	15	16	17	18
3	22	28	33	39	45	50	56	61	67	73	78	84	89	95	100
4	30	37	45	52	60	67	74	82	89	97	104	112	119	126	134
5	37	47	56	65	74	84	93	102	112	121	130	140	149	158	167
6	45	56	67	78	89	100	112	123	134	145	156	167	179	190	201
7	52	65	78	91	104	117	130	143	156	169	187	195	208	231	234
8	59	74	89	104	119	134	149	164	179	193	208	223	238	253	268
9	67	84	100	117	134	151	167	184	201	218	234	251	268	285	301
10	74	93	112	130	149	167	186	205	223	242	260	279	298	316	335
11	82	102	123	143	164	184	205	225	245	266	286	307	327	348	368
12	89	112	134	156	179	201	223	246	268	290	312	335	357	379	402
13	97	121	145	169	193	218	242	266	290	314	339	363	387	411	435
14	104	130	156	182	208	234	260	286	312	339	365	391	417	443	469
15	112	140	167	195	223	251	279	307	335	363	391	419	446	474	502
16	119	149	179	208	238	268	298	327	357	387	417	446	476	506	536
17	126	158	190	221	253	285	316	348	379	411	423	474	506	538	569
18	134	167	201	234	268	301	335	368	402	435	469	502	536	569	603
19	141	177	212	247	283	318	353	389	424	459	495	530	565	601	636
20	149	186	223	260	298	335	372	409	446	484	521	558	595	632	670
21	156	195	234	273	312	352	391	430	469	508	547	586	625	664	703
22	164	205	246	286	327	368	409	450	491	532	573	614	655	696	737
23	171	214	257	299	342	385	428	471	513	556	599	642	684	727	770
24	179	223	268	312	357	402	446	491	536	580	625	670	714	759	804

Food buying guide: Fish and shellfish

Food item and form	Market unit	Approximate servings per market unit*	Approximate weight per cup (Grams)	(Ounces)
Fish, fresh or frozen				
whole	1 lb.	1½		
chunks	1 lb.	3		
dressed	1 lb.	2⅓		
fillets	1 lb.	3⅓		
steaks	1 lb	3		
cakes, frozen	1 lb.	5⅓		
portions, unbreaded, frozen	1 lb.	4		
portions, breaded, fried or raw, frozen	1 lb.	5⅓		
sticks, frozen	1 lb.	5⅓		
Fish, canned				
gefilte fish	1 lb.	3	162	5.7
mackerel	15 oz.	4¼	182	6.4
Maine sardines	12 oz.	3¾	160	5.6
salmon	1 lb.	4¼	168	5.9
tuna	7 oz.	2	170	6.0
Fish, cured				
lox	1 lb.	5⅓		
salt fish	1 lb.	5⅓		
smoked fish	1 lb.	3½		
Shellfish				
Clams, fresh or frozen				
in shell (hard)	1 doz.	2		
in shell (soft)	1 doz.	1		
shucked	1 lb.	2½		
frozen, breaded, raw	1 lb.	4½		
Clams, canned, minced	7½ oz.	2½	158	5.6
Crabs, fresh or frozen				
in shell (Blue)	1 lb.	¾		
in shell (Dungeness)	1 lb.	1¼		
meat	1 lb.	5	163	5.7
cakes, frozen	1 lb.	5		
legs and sections, frozen	1 lb.	2½		
deviled, frozen	1 lb.	5⅓		
Crab meat, canned	6½ oz.	1¾		
Lobster, fresh or frozen				
in shell	1 lb.	1¼		
meat	1 lb.	4¾	154	5.4
spiny tails, frozen	1 lb.	2⅔		

Food item and form	Market unit	Approximate servings per market unit*	Approximate weight per cup (Grams)	(Ounces)
Oysters, fresh or frozen				
in shell	1 doz.	2		
shucked	1 lb.	2	235	8.3
breaded, frozen	1 lb.	4⅔		
Oysters, canned, whole	5 oz.	1⅔	156	5.5
Scallops, fresh or frozen				
shucked	1 lb.	3⅓		
breaded, frozen	1 lb.	4		
Shrimp, fresh or frozen				
in shell	1 lb.	2⅔		
raw, peeled	1 lb.	3⅓		
cooked, peeled, cleaned	1 lb.	5⅓		
breaded, frozen	1 lb.	4½		
Shrimp, canned	13¼ oz.	4⅓	129	4.6

*One serving equals 3 ounces of cooked boneless fish or shellfish.

Source: *Handbook of Food Preparation,* American Home Economics Association.

Food buying guide: Fruits

Food item and form	Market unit	Approximate volume or pieces per market unit	Approximate weight per cup* (Grams	(Ounces)
Apples				
fresh, whole	1 lb.	3 medium		
pared and sliced		2¾c.	122	4.3
sauce, sweetened (not canned)		1¾ c.	252	8.9
frozen, sliced, sweetened	20 oz.	2½ c.	205	7.2
canned, sliced	20 oz.	2½ c.	204	7.5
juice	46 fl oz.	5¾ c.	249	8.8
sauce	1 lb.	1¾ c.	259	9.1
dried	1 lb.	4⅓ c.	104	3.7
cooked		8 c.	244	8.6
Apricots				
fresh, whole	1 lb.	8–12	115	4.1
sliced or halved		2½ c.	156	5.5
canned, whole (medium)	1 lb.	8–12	225	7.9
halved (medium)	1 lb.	12–20 halves	217	7.7
dried	11 oz.	2¼ c.	150	5.3
cooked, fruit and liquid		4⅓ c.	285	10.0
Avocados				
fresh	1 lb.			
sliced, diced, wedges		2½ c.	142	5.0
Bananas				
fresh, whole	1 lb.	3–4		
sliced		2 c.	142	5.0
mashed		1⅓ c.	232	8.2
dried	1 lb.	4½ c.	100	3.5
Blueberries				
fresh	1 lb.	2 c.	146	5.2
frozen	10 oz.	1½ c.	161	5.7
canned	14 oz.	1½ c.	170	6.0
Cherries				
fresh, red, pitted	1 lb.	2⅓ c.	154	5.4
frozen, red, tart, pitted	20 oz.	2 c.	242	8.5
canned, red, tart, pitted	1 lb.	1½ c.	177	6.2
sweet, unpitted	1 lb.	1¾ c.	177	6.2
Cranberries				
fresh, uncooked	1 lb.	4 c.	151	5.3
sauce		4 c.	215	7.6
canned, sauce	1 lb.	1⅔ c.	278	9.8
juice	1 qt.	4 c.	250	8.8

Food item and form	Market unit	Approximate volume or pieces per market unit	Approximate weight per cup* (Grams	(Ounces)
Currants				
dried	1 lb.	3¼ c.	140	4.9
Dates				
dried, whole	1 lb.	60 dates		
pitted, cut	1 lb.	2½ c.	178	6.3
Figs				
fresh	1 lb.	12 medium		
canned	1 lb.	12–16 figs	230	8.1
dried, whole	1 lb.	44 figs		
cut fine		2⅔ c.	168	5.9
Fruit juice				
frozen	6 fl. oz.	¾ c.		
canned	46 fl. oz.	5¾ c.	247	8.7
Fruits				
mixed, frozen	12 oz.	1⅓ c.		
canned, cocktail or salad	17 oz.	2 c.	229	8.1
Grapefruit				
fresh	1 lb.	1 medium		
sections		1 c.	194	6.8
frozen, sections	13½ oz.	1½ c.	219	7.7
canned, sections	16 oz.	2 c.	241	8.5
Grapes, fresh				
seeded	1 lb.	2 c.	184	6.5
seedless	1 lb.	2½ c.	169	6.0
Lemons				
fresh	3 lb.	1 doz.		
juice		2 c.	247	8.7
frozen, juice	6 fl oz.	¾ c.	283	10.0
canned, juice	8 fl oz.	1 c.	245	8.6
Melon				
frozen, balls	12 oz.	1½ c.	231	8.2
Oranges				
fresh	6 lb.	1 doz.		
diced or sectioned		12 c.	214	7.5
juice		4 c.	247	8.7
frozen, juice, reconstituted	6 fl oz.	3 c.	268	9.5
canned, juice	46 fl oz.	5¾ c.	247	8.7
canned, mandarin, fruit and juice	11 oz.	1¼ c.	250	8.8

Food item and form	Market unit	Approximate volume or pieces per market unit	Approximate weight per cup* (Grams)	(Ounces)
Peaches				
fresh	1 lb.	4 medium		
sliced		2 c.	177	6.2
frozen, slices and juice	10 oz.	1⅛ c.	251	8.8
canned, halves	1 lb.	6–10 halves	224	7.9
slices	1 lb.	2 c.	218	7.7
dried	1 lb.	3 c.	160	5.6
cooked		6 c.	244	8.6
Pears				
fresh	1 lb.	4 medium		
sliced		2⅛ c.	213	7.5
canned, halves	1 lb.	6–10 halves	227	8.0
Pineapple				
fresh	2 lb.	1 medium		
cubed		3 c.	146	5.2
frozen, chunks	13½ oz.	1½ c.	204	7.2
canned, chunks, tidbits	29 oz.	3¾ c.	198	7.0
crushed	29 oz.	3¾ c.	260	9.2
sliced	20 oz.	10 slices	208	7.3
juice	46 fl oz.	5¾ c.		
Plums				
fresh	1 lb.	8–20 plums		
halved		2 c.	185	6.5
canned, whole	1 lb.	10–14 plums	223	7.9
Prunes				
canned	1 lb.	10–14 prunes	196	6.9
dried, whole	1 lb.	2½ c.	176	6.2
cooked		4–4½ c.	229	8.1
pitted	1 lb.	2¼ c.	162	5.7
cooked		4–4½ c.	210	7.4
Raisins				
seeded, whole	1 lb.	3¼ c.	142	5.0
chopped		2½ c.	182	6.4
seedless, whole	1 lb.	2¾ c.	146	5.2
cooked		2¾ c.	183	6.5
chopped		2 c.	189	6.7
Rhubarb				
fresh	1 lb.	4–8 pieces		
cut			122	4.3
cooked		2 c.	242	8.5
frozen, sliced	12 oz.	1½ c.	168	5.9

Food item and form	Market unit	Approximate volume or pieces per market unit	Approximate weight per cup* (Grams	(Ounces)
Strawberries				
fresh, whole	1½ lb.	4 c.	144	5.1
sliced		4 c.	148	5.2
frozen, whole	1 lb.	1⅓ c.	204	7.2
sliced or halved	10 oz.	1 c.	235	8.3

*Weight per cup is that of food alone without liquid, unless otherwise noted.
Source: *Handbook of Food Preparation,* American Home Economics Association.

Food buying guide: Meat

Food item and form	Market unit	Approximate volume or number of servings per market unit*	Approximate weight per cup (Grams)	(Ounces)
Meat, fresh or frozen				
boned or ground	1 lb.		227	8.0
cooked		3–4 servings		
diced		1½–2 c.	142	5.0
with minimum amount of bone (steaks, roasts, chops, etc.)	1 lb.			
cooked		2–3 servings		
diced		1–1½ c.	142	5.0
with large amount of bone (shoulder cuts, short ribs, neck, etc.)	1 lb.			
cooked		1–2 servings		
diced		1 c.	142	5.0
Cured and/or smoked				
ham, ground	1 lb.		170	6.0
cooked, ground		2½–3 servings	109	3.8
diced		1½–2 c.	147	5.2
bacon	1 lb.	24 slices		
frankfurters	1 lb.	8–10 pieces		
luncheon meat, sliced	12 oz.	8 slices		
diced			141	5.0
Canned				
corned beef	12 oz.	4 servings		
ham, smoked	1½ lb.	6–8 servings		
diced		3¾–4½ c.		
luncheon meat	12 oz.	4 servings		
sausage, Vienna	4 oz.	8–10 sausages		
Dried				
chipped beef	4 oz.	1⅔ servings		

*3 ounces of cooked meat is the usual amount for one serving.

Source: *Handbook of Food Preparation,* American Home Economics Association.

Food buying guide: Poultry

Food item and form	Market unit	Approximate volume or number of servings per market unit*	Approximate weight per cup (Grams)	(Ounces)
Chicken, ready-to-cook				
broiler-fryer	1½–3½ lb.	2–4 servings		
roaster	1 lb.	2¼ servings		
Rock Cornish hen	Under 2 lbs.	1–2 servings		
stewing	1 lb.			
cooked, boned		2½ servings		
diced		1½ c.	136	4.8
ground			113	4.0
canned, boned	5–6 oz.	1½–2 servings		
Duck, ready-to-cook	1 lb.	2–2½ servings		
Goose, ready-to-cook	1 lb.	2–2⅔ servings		
Turkey, ready-to-cook	1 lb.			
cooked, boned, diced		1–2 servings	133	4.7
canned, boned	5 oz.	1½ servings		

*Amounts are based on 3 ounces of cooked poultry meat without bone per serving.
Source: *Handbook of Food Preparation,* American Home Economics Association.

Food buying guide: Vegetables

Food item and form	Market unit	Approximate volume or pieces per market unit	Approximate weight per cup* (Grams)	(Ounces)
Asparagus, spears				
fresh	1 lb.	16–20		
cooked		2 c.	181	6.4
canned	14½–16 oz.	12–18	195	6.9
frozen spears, cuts, and tips	10 oz.	2 c.	181	6.4
Beans, green				
fresh	1 lb.	3 c.	114	4.0
cooked		2½ c.	125	4.4
frozen	9 oz.	1½ c.	161	5.7
canned	15½ oz.	1¾ c.	135	4.8
Beans, kidney, canned	16–17 oz.	2 c.	187	6.6
dried	1 lb.	2½ c.	184	6.5
cooked		5½ c.	185	6.5
Beans, lima, shelled				
fresh	1 lb.	2 c.	155	5.5
cooked		1⅔–2 c.	166	5.9
frozen	10 oz.	1¾ c.	173	6.1
canned	16 oz.	2 c.	170	6.0
dried	1 lb.	2½ c.	180	6.3
cooked		5½ c.	186	6.6
Beans, navy, dried	1 lb.	2⅓ c.	190	6.7
cooked		5½ c.	191	6.7
Beans, soybeans, dried	1 lb.	2 c.	210	7.4
Beets, without tops				
fresh	1 lb.	2 c.	145	5.1
cooked		2 c.	180	6.3
canned	16–17 oz.	2 c.	167	5.9
Broccoli, fresh, cooked	1 lb.	2 c.	164	5.8
Broccoli, spears, chopped, frozen	10 oz.	1½ c.	188	6.6
Brussels sprouts				
fresh	1 lb.	4 c.	102	3.6
cooked		2½ c.	180	6.4
frozen	10 oz.	18–24 sprouts		
Cabbage				
fresh	1 lb.			
shredded		3½–4½ c.	80	2.8
cooked		2 c.	146	5.2

Food item and form	Market unit	Approximate volume or pieces per market unit	Approximate weight per cup* (Grams)	(Ounces)
Carrots, without tops				
fresh	1 lb.	3 c.	130	4.6
shredded		2½ c.	112	4.0
diced			137	4.8
cooked		2–2½ c.	160	5.6
frozen	1 lb.			
cooked		2½ c.	165	5.8
canned	16 oz.	2 c.	159	5.6
Cauliflower, fresh	1 lb.	1½ c.	104	3.7
cooked		1½ c.	125	4.4
frozen	10 oz.	2 c.	152	5.4
cooked		1½ c.	179	6.3
Celery, fresh	1 lb.	2 bunches	121	4.3
cooked		2–2½ c.	153	5.4
Corn, fresh ears	1 doz.			
cooked		2½ c.	165	5.8
frozen, cut	10 oz.	1¾ c.	135	4.8
cooked		1½–2 c.	182	6.4
canned, cream style	16–17 oz.	2 c.	249	8.8
whole kernel	12 oz.	1½ c.	169	6.0
Eggplant, fresh	1 lb.			
diced		2½ c.	99	3.5
cooked		2½ c.	213	7.5
Greens, fresh	1 lb.		77	2.7
cooked		4–6 c.	190	6.7
frozen	10 oz.	1½–2 c.	187	6.6
Lentils, dried	1 lb.	2¼ c.	191	6.7
cooked		5 c.	202	7.1
Lettuce, head	1 lb.	6¼ c.		
leaf	1 lb.	6¼ c.		
romaine	1 lb.	6 c.		
endive	1 lb.	4¼ c.		
Mixed vegetables, frozen	10 oz.	2 c.	182	6.4
canned	16–17 oz.	2 c.	179	6.3
Mushrooms, fresh, sliced	1 lb.	2–3 c.	68	2.4
canned	4 oz.	⅔ c.	161	5.7
Okra, fresh, cooked	1 lb.	2¼ c.	177	6.2
frozen	10 oz.	1¼ c.	209	7.4
canned	15½ oz.	1¾ c.	171	6.0

Food item and form	Market unit	Approximate volume or pieces per market unit	Approximate weight per cup* (Grams)	(Ounces)
Onions, fresh	1 lb.	3 large		
chopped		2–2½ c.	135	4.8
cooked			197	6.9
frozen, chopped	12 oz.	3 c.		
canned	16–17 oz.	2 c.		
dried			64	2.3
Parsnips, fresh	1 lb.	4 medium		
cooked		2 c.	211	7.4
Peas, green, fresh, in pod	1 lb.			
shelled		1 c.	138	4.9
cooked		1 c.	163	5.7
frozen	10 oz.	2 c.	156	5.5
cooked		2 c.	167	5.9
canned	1 lb.	2 c.	168	5.9
dried, split	1 lb.	2¼ c.	200	7.1
cooked		5 c.	194	6.8
Peas, black-eyed, fresh	1 lb.		144	5.1
cooked		2⅓ c.	162	5.7
frozen, cooked	10 oz.	1½ c.	171	6.0
canned	16–17 oz.	2 c.	205	7.2
dried, split	1 lb.		200	7.1
cooked			248	8.7
Potatoes, white, fresh	1 lb.	3 medium	164	5.8
cooked, diced, or sliced		2¼ c.	163	5.7
mashed		1¾ c.	207	7.3
frozen, French fried or puffs	9 oz.	3–4		
canned, whole	16–17 oz.	8–12	179	6.3
dried flakes	6–7 oz.	4½ c.	36	1.3
reconstituted		10¾ c.	212	7.5
dried granules	1 lb.	2¼ c.	201	7.1
reconstituted		10½ c.	212	7.5
Pumpkin, fresh, cooked, mashed	1 lb.	1 c.	247	8.7
canned	16–17 oz.	2 c.	244	8.6
Radishes, sliced	6 oz.	1¼ c.		
Rutabaga, fresh, cubed	1 lb.	2½ c.	139	4.9
cooked		2 c.	163	5.7
Sauerkraut, canned	15–16 oz.	2 c.	188	6.6
Spinach, fresh	1 lb.	4 c.	54	1.9
cooked		1½ c.	200	7.1
frozen	10 oz.	1½ c.	190	6.7
canned	15 oz.	2 c.	221	7.8

Food item and form	Market unit	Approximate volume or pieces per market unit	Approximate weight per cup* (Grams)	(Ounces)
Squash, winter, fresh	1 lb.			
cooked, mashed		1 c.	244	8.6
frozen	12 oz.	1½ c.	242	8.5
canned	15–16 oz.	1¾–2 c.		
Squash, summer, fresh	1 lb.		136	4.8
cooked, mashed		1⅔ c.	238	8.4
frozen, sliced	10 oz.	1½ c.	211	7.4
canned	1 lb.			
Sweet potatoes, fresh	1 lb.	3 medium		
cooked, sliced			232	8.2
frozen	12 oz.	3–4	200	7.1
canned	16–17 oz.	1¾–2 c.	220	7.8
dried, flakes	1 lb.		115	4.1
reconstituted			255	9.0
Tomatoes, fresh	1 lb.	3–4 small	162	5.7
cooked		1½ c.		
canned, whole	16 oz.	2 c.	238	8.4
sauce	8 oz.	1 c.	258	9.1
Turnips, fresh	1 lb.	3 medium	134	4.7
cooked		2 c.	196	6.9

*Weight per cup is that of food alone without liquid.

Source: *Handbook of Food Preparation,* American Home Economics Association.

Food buying guide equivalents: fresh vs. packaged

Commodity	Unit	Approximate equivalent
Apples	1 pound dried	8 pounds fresh
	1 pound chopped	5 pounds fresh
	1 case canned	1.4 bushels fresh
Applesauce	1 case canned	1.2 bushels fresh
Apricots	1 pound dried	6 pounds fresh
Barley flour	100 pounds	4.59 bushels barley
Beans, lima	1 pound shelled	2 pounds unshelled
Beans, snap or wax	1 case canned	0.008 ton fresh
Buckwheat flour	100 pounds	3.47 bushels buckwheat
Calves	1 pound live weight	0.557 pound dressed weight
Cattle	1 pound live weight	0.561 pound dressed weight
Cane syrup	1 gallon	5 pounds sugar
Cherries, tart	1 case canned	0.023 ton fresh
Chickens	1 pound live weight	0.72 pound ready-to-cook weight
Corn, shelled	1 bushel (56 lbs.)	2 bushels (70 pounds) of husked ear corn
Corn, sweet	1 case canned	0.03 ton fresh
Cornmeal:		
Degermed	100 pounds	3.16 bushels corn
Cotton	1 pound ginned	3.26 pounds seed cotton, including trash
Cottonseed meal	1 pound	2.1 pounds cottonseed
Cottonseed oil	1 pound	5.88 pounds cottonseed
Dairy products:		
Butter	1 pound	21.1 pounds milk
Cheese	1 pound	10 pounds milk
Condensed milk, whole	1 pound	2.3 pounds milk
Dry cream	1 pound	19 pounds milk
Dry milk, whole	1 pound	7.6 pounds milk
Evaporated milk, whole	1 pound	2.14 pounds milk
Malted milk	1 pound	2.6 pounds milk
Nonfat dry milk	1 pound	11 pounds liquid skim milk
Ice cream	1 gallon	15 pounds milk
Ice cream (eliminating fat from butter and concentrated milk)	1 gallon	12 pounds milk
Eggs	1 case	47 pounds
Eggs, shell	1 case	39.5 pounds frozen or liquid whole eggs
Eggs, shell	1 case	10.3 pounds dried whole eggs

Commodity	Unit	Approximate equivalent
Figs	1 pound dried	3 pounds fresh in California; 4 pounds fresh elsewhere
Flaxseed	1 bushel	About 2½ gallons oil
Grapefruit, Florida	1 case canned juice	0.64 box fresh fruit
Hogs	1 pound live weight	0.579 pound dressed weight, excluding lard
Linseed meal	1 pound	1.51 pounds flaxseed
Linseed oil	1 pound	2.77 pounds flaxseed
Malt	1 bushel (34 lbs.)	1 bushel barley (48 lbs.)
Maple syrup	1 gallon	8 pounds maple sugar
Nuts:		
Almonds, imported	1 pound shelled	3⅓ pounds unshelled
Almonds, California	1 pound shelled	2 pounds unshelled
Brazil	1 pound shelled	2 pounds unshelled
Cashews	1 pound shelled	4.55 pounds unshelled
Chestnuts	1 pound shelled	1.19 pounds unshelled
Filberts	1 pound shelled	2.5 pounds unshelled
Pecans:		
Seedling	1 pound shelled	2.78 pounds unshelled
Improved	1 pound shelled	2.5 pounds unshelled
Pignolias	1 pound shelled	1.3 pounds unshelled
Pistachios	1 pound shelled	2 pounds unshelled
Walnuts:		
Black	1 pound shelled	5.88 pounds unshelled
Persian (English)	1 pound shelled	2.67 pounds unshelled
Oatmeal	100 pounds	7.6 bushels oats
Oranges, Florida	1 case canned juice	0.53 box fresh
Peaches, California, freestone	1 pound dried	6.5 pounds fresh
Peaches, California, clingstone	1 pound dried	7½ pounds fresh
Peaches, clingstone	1 case canned	1 bushel fresh
	1 case canned	0.023 ton fresh
Peanuts	1 pound shelled	1½ pounds unshelled
Pears	1 pound dried	6½ pounds fresh
Pears, Bartlett	1 case canned	1.1 bushels fresh
	1 case canned	0.026 ton fresh
Peas, green	1 pound shelled	2½ pounds unshelled
	1 case canned	0.009 ton fresh (shelled)
Prunes	1 pound dried	2.7 pounds fresh in California; 3 to 4 pounds
	1 pound	4.3 pounds fresh grapes

Commodity	Unit	Approximate equivalent
Rice, milled (excluding brewers)	100 pounds	152 pounds rough or unhulled rice
Rye flour	100 pounds	2.23 bushels rye beginning 1947
Sheep and lambs	1 pound live weight	0.482 pound dressed weight (1954-63 average)
Soybean meal	1 pound	1.27 pounds soybeans
Soybean oil	1 pound	5.49 pounds soybeans
Sugar	1 ton raw	0.9346 ton refined
Tobacco	1 pound farm-sales weight	Various weights of stemmed and unstemmed, according to aging and the type of tobacco. (See circular 435, U.S. Dept. of Agr.)
Tomatoes	1 case canned	0.018 ton fresh
Turkeys	1 pound live weight	0.8 pound ready-to-cook weight
Wheat flour	100 pounds	2.3 bushels wheat
Wool, domestic apparel shorn	1 pound greasy	0.48 pound scoured
Wool, domestic apparel pulled	1 pound greasy	0.73 pound scoured

Source: U.S. Department of Agriculture.

Food buying guide: weights of common cooking commodities

Food	Weight per cup in dry (packaged) ounces
Beans (dry)	6½
Butter, margarine, cooking oils	8
Citrus fruit juice (fresh)	8½
Cornflakes	1
Cornmeal	5
Eggs (whole)	8½
Flour (wheat, all-purpose, sifted)	4
Flour (cake, sifted)	3½
Milk (whole, fluid)	8½
Milk (dry)	4½
Nutmeats (pecan)	4
Oatmeal	3
Pancake mix	5
Prunes (dried)	5½

Food	Weight per cup in dry (packaged) ounces
Raisins (seedless)	5
Rice	7
Shortening (vegetable)	7
Sugar (brown, moist, firmly packed)	7½
Sugar (granulated)	7

Source: *Special Publication 430,* National Bureau of Standards.

Food temperatures for safety

Bacterial growth in food causes spoilage and food poisoning. It can be stopped or slowed at proper temperatures.

Temperature (Degrees Fahrenheit)	Use and effect on bacteria
240–250	Canning temperature for low-acid vegetables, meat, and poultry in pressure canner to kill most bacteria.
212–240	Canning temperatures for fruits, tomatoes, and pickles in water-bath canner to kill most bacteria.
165–212	Cooking temperatures that destroy most bacteria. (The time required to kill bacteria decreases as temperature increases.)
140–165	Warming temperatures that prevent growth of bacteria, but do not kill many of them.
125–140	Some bacteria grow; many survive.
60–125	*Danger Zone.* Rapid growth of bacteria and production of toxins take place. Do not keep food at this temperature for more than 2 to 3 hours.
40–60	Some growth of food poisoning bacteria may occur.
32–40	Some bacteria that cause food spoilage can grow. (Do not store raw meats for more than 5 days or poultry, fish, and ground meat for more than 2 days, in the refrigerator at these temperatures.)
0–32	Bacteria growth is halted, although many strains can survive. (Do not store food at temperatures above 10°F. for more than a few weeks.)

Source: U.S. Department of Agriculture.

Frozen food maximum storage periods

To maintain good quality and food safety, use up frozen foods before these periods have elapsed.

Food	Approximate holding period at 0° F (Months)
Fruits and vegetables	
Fruits	
Cherries	12
Peaches	12
Raspberries	12
Strawberries	12
Fruit juice concentrates:	
Apple	12
Grape	12
Orange	12
Vegetables:	
Asparagus	8
Beans	8
Cauliflower	8
Corn	8
Peas	8
Spinach	8
Baked goods	
Bread and yeast rolls:	
White bread	3
Cinnamon rolls	2
Plain rolls	3
Cakes:	
Angel	2
Chiffon	2
Chocolate layer	4
Fruit	12
Pound	6
Yellow	6
Danish pastry	3
Doughnuts:	
Cake type	3
Yeast raised	3
Pies (unbaked):	
Apple	8
Boysenberry	8

Food	Approximate holding period at 0° F (Months)
Cherry	8
Peach	8
Meat	
Beef:	
Hamburger or chipped (thin) steaks	4
Roasts	12
Steaks	12
Lamb:	
Patties (ground meat)	4
Roasts	9
Pork, cured	2
Pork, fresh:	
Chops	4
Roasts	8
Sausage	2
Veal:	
Cutlets, chops	9
Roasts	9
Cooked meat:	
Meal dinners	3
Meat pie	3
Swiss steak	3
Poultry	
Chicken:	
Cut-up	9
Livers	3
Whole	12
Duck, whole	6
Goose, whole	6
Turkey:	
Cut-up	6
Whole	12
Cooked chicken and turkey:	
Chicken or turkey dinners (sliced meat and gravy)	6
Chicken or turkey pies	6
Fried chicken	4
Fried chicken dinners	4

Food	Approximate holding period at 0° F (Months)
Fish and shellfish	
Fish fillets:	
Cod, flounder, haddock, halibut, pollack	6
Mullet, ocean perch, sea trout, striped bass	3
Pacific Ocean perch	2
Salmon steaks	2
Sea trout, dressed	3
Striped bass, dressed	3
Whiting, drawn	4
Clams, shucked	3
Crab meat:	
Dungeness	3
King	10
Oysters, shucked	4
Shrimp	12
Cooked fish and shellfish:	
Fish with cheese sauce	3
Fish with lemon butter sauce	3
Fried fish dinner	3
Fried fish sticks, scallops, or shrimp	3
Shrimp creole	3
Tuna pie	3
Frozen desserts	
Ice cream	1
Sherbet	1

Source: *Yearbook,* U.S. Department of Agriculture, 1973.

Fuel cost comparisons

It is impossible to compare the cost of a gallon of fuel oil with 100 cubic feet of natural gas until you convert both into comparable units. The standard unit of comparison is the *therm,* which equals 100,000 BTUs of heat energy. Not all stoves operate at identical efficiencies; the chart below takes into account the average efficiency of a furnace (as noted) using each type of fuel. (Rounding off has led to minor inconsistencies.) Using the chart, if a gallon of fuel oil costs 20 cents, and the heat from 100 cu. ft. of natural gas costs 10 cents, their prices are comparable.

	Cost per therm ($)					
	Natural gas	**Oil**	**LP gas**	**LP gas**	**Electric**	**Wood**
Efficiency of furnace	65%	60%	65%	65%	100%	50%
Standard unit	100 cu.ft.	gallon	gallon	pound	kilowatt hour	cord
	.10	.20	.10			.20
	.20	.40	.20	.05	.01	.40
	.40	.60	.40		.02	.60
	.50	.70	.50	.10	.03	.80
	.60	.80	.60	.15		1.00
	.80	1.00	.70		.04	1.20
	.90	1.20	.80	.20	.05	1.40
	1.00	1.40	1.00			1.60
	1.20	1.60	1.10	.25	.06	1.80
	1.30	1.70	1.20		.07	2.00
	1.40	1:80	1.30	.30		2.20
	1.60	2.00	1.40	.35	.08	2.40
	1.70	2.20	1.50		.09	2.60
	1.80	2.40	1.60	.40	.10	2.80

Source: *Energy Conserving Window Treatments,* University of Wisconsin Extension.

Fruit and vegetable availability

0=Supplies scarce or nonexistent.
1=Supplies moderate.
2=Supplies plentiful.
3=Supplies exceptionally abundant.

Produce	Jan	Feb	Mar	Apr	May	June	July	Aug	Sept	Oct	Nov	Dec
Apples	2	2	2	2	2	1	1	1	2	2	2	2
Apricots	0	0	0	0	1	3	3	0	0	0	0	0
Artichokes	1	1	2	2	2	1	1	1	1	1	1	1
Asparagus	0	1	3	3	2	1	0	0	0	0	0	0
Avocados	2	2	2	2	2	2	2	2	2	2	2	2
Bananas	2	2	2	2	2	2	2	2	2	2	2	2
Beans (Snap)	1	1	1	1	2	2	2	2	1	1	1	1
Beets	1	1	1	1	1	2	2	2	2	2	1	1
Berries (Misc.)	0	0	0	0	0	3	3	1	0	0	0	0
Blueberries	0	0	0	0	0	3	3	2	1	0	0	0
Broccoli	2	2	2	2	1	1	1	1	1	2	2	2
Brussels sprouts	2	2	1	1	1	0	0	0	1	2	2	2
Cabbage	2	2	2	2	2	2	2	2	2	2	2	2
Cantaloupes	0	0	0	0	2	3	3	3	2	2	0	0
Carrots	2	2	2	2	2	2	2	2	2	2	2	2
Cauliflower	1	1	1	1	1	1	1	1	2	2	2	1
Celery	2	2	2	2	2	2	2	2	2	2	2	2
Cherries	0	0	0	0	1	3	3	1	0	0	0	0
Chinese cabbage	1	1	1	1	1	1	1	1	1	1	1	1
Corn, sweet	0	0	1	1	2	2	2	2	2	1	1	0
Cranberries	1	0	0	0	0	0	0	0	1	2	3	2
Cucumbers	2	2	2	2	2	2	2	2	2	2	2	2
Eggplant	1	1	1	1	1	1	1	2	2	2	1	1
Escarole/Endive	2	2	2	2	2	2	2	2	2	2	2	2
Endive (Belgian)	1	1	1	1	1	0	0	0	0	1	1	1
Grapefruit	2	2	2	2	2	1	1	1	1	1	2	2
Grapes	0	0	0	0	1	1	2	3	3	3	2	1
Greens	2	2	2	2	2	2	2	2	2	2	2	2
Honeydews	0	0	0	0	1	2	2	3	3	2	1	0
Lemons	2	2	2	2	2	2	2	2	2	2	2	2
Lettuce	2	2	2	2	2	2	2	2	2	2	2	2
Limes	1	1	1	1	1	2	2	2	1	1	1	1
Mushrooms	1	1	1	1	1	1	1	1	1	1	1	1
Nectarines	0	0	0	0	0	1	3	3	1	0	0	0
Okra	0	0	1	1	1	1	1	1	1	1	0	0
Onions (Dry)	2	2	2	2	2	2	2	2	2	2	2	2
Onions (Green)	1	1	2	2	2	2	2	2	2	1	1	1
Oranges	2	2	2	2	2	2	1	1	1	2	2	2

Produce	Jan	Feb	Mar	Apr	May	June	July	Aug	Sept	Oct	Nov	Dec
Parsley	1	1	1	1	1	1	1	1	1	1	2	2
Parsnips	1	1	1	1	1	0	0	0	1	1	1	1
Peaches	0	0	0	0	1	2	3	3	2	0	0	0
Pears	1	1	1	1	1	0	1	2	2	2	2	1
Peppers (Sweet)	2	2	2	2	2	2	2	2	2	2	2	2
Pineapples	1	1	2	2	2	2	1	1	1	1	1	1
Plums/Prunes	0	0	0	0	0	1	3	3	2	1	0	0
Potatoes	2	2	2	2	2	2	2	2	2	2	2	2
Radishes	2	2	2	2	2	2	2	2	2	2	2	2
Rhubarb	1	1	1	1	3	1	0	0	0	0	0	0
Spinach	2	2	2	2	2	1	1	1	1	1	1	1
Squash	2	2	2	2	2	2	2	2	2	2	2	2
Strawberries	1	1	2	3	3	3	2	1	1	1	1	1
Sweet potatoes	2	2	2	2	1	1	1	1	2	2	3	2
Tangerines	2	0	0	0	0	0	0	0	0	0	1	3
Tomatoes	2	2	2	2	2	2	2	2	2	2	2	2
Turnips	1	1	1	1	1	1	1	1	1	1	1	1
Watermelons	0	0	0	1	2	3	3	2	1	1	0	0

Source: U.S. Department of Agriculture.

Garden planting: earliest dates

These are recommended earliest dates for getting your seeds or transplants into the ground. If you don't know local frost dates, contact your County Extension Agent.

Crop	Planting dates for localities in which average date of last freeze is— Jan. 30	Feb. 8	Feb. 18	Feb. 28	Mar. 10	Mar. 20	Mar. 30
Asparagus[1]					Jan. 1–Mar. 1	Feb. 1–Mar. 10	Feb. 15–Mar. 20
Beans, lima	Feb. 1–Apr. 15	Feb. 10–May 1	Mar. 1–May 1	Mar. 15–June 1	Mar. 20–June 1	Apr. 1–June 15	Apr. 15–June 20
Beans, snap	Feb. 1–Apr. 1	Feb. 1–May 1	Mar. 1–May 1	Mar. 10–May 15	Mar. 15–May 15	Mar. 15–May 25	Apr. 1–June 1
Beets	Jan. 1–Mar. 15	Jan. 10–Mar. 15	Jan. 20–Apr. 1	Feb. 1–Apr. 15	Feb. 15–June 1	Feb. 15–May 15	Mar. 1–June 1
Broccoli, sprouting[1]	Jan. 1–30	Jan. 1–30	Jan. 15–Feb. 15	Feb. 1–Mar. 1	Feb. 15–Mar. 15	Feb. 15–Mar. 15	Mar. 1–20
Brussels sprouts[1]	Jan. 1–30	Jan. 1–30	Jan. 15–Feb. 15	Feb. 1–Mar. 1	Feb. 15–Mar. 15	Feb. 15–Mar. 15	Mar. 1–20
Cabbage[1]	Jan. 1–15	Jan. 1–Feb. 10	Jan. 1–Feb. 25	Jan. 15–Feb. 25	Jan. 25–Mar. 1	Feb. 1–Mar. 1	Feb. 15–Mar. 10
Cabbage, Chinese	(2)	(2)	(2)	(2)	(2)	(2)	(2)
Carrots	Jan. 1–Mar. 1	Jan. 1–Mar. 1	Jan. 15–Mar. 1	Feb. 1–Mar. 1	Feb. 10–Mar. 15	Feb. 15–Mar. 20	Mar. 1–Apr. 10
Cauliflower[1]	Jan. 1–Feb. 1	Jan. 1–Feb. 1	Jan. 10–Feb. 10	Jan. 20–Feb. 20	Feb. 1–Mar. 1	Feb. 10–Mar. 10	Feb. 20–Mar. 20
Celery and celeriac	Jan. 1–Feb. 1	Jan. 10–Feb. 10	Jan. 20–Feb. 20	Feb. 1–Mar. 1	Feb. 20–Mar. 20	Mar. 1–Apr. 1	Mar. 15–Apr. 15
Chard	Jan. 1–Apr. 1	Jan. 10–Apr. 1	Jan. 20–Apr. 15	Feb. 1–May 1	Feb. 15–May 15	Feb. 20–May 15	Mar. 1–May 25
Chervil and chives	Jan. 1–Feb. 1	Jan. 1–Feb. 1	Jan. 1–Feb. 1	Jan. 15–Feb. 15	Feb. 1–Mar. 1	Feb. 10–Mar. 10	Feb. 15–Mar. 15
Chicory, witloof					June 1–July 1	June 1–July 1	June 1–July 1
Collards[1]	Jan. 1–Feb. 15	Jan. 1–Feb. 15	Jan. 1–Mar. 15	Jan. 15–Mar. 15	Feb. 1–Apr. 1	Feb. 15–May 1	Mar. 1–June 1
Cornsalad	Jan. 1–Feb. 15	Jan. 1–Feb. 15	Jan. 1–Mar. 15	Jan. 1–Mar. 1	Jan. 1–Mar. 15	Jan. 1–Mar. 15	Jan. 15–Mar. 15
Corn, sweet	Feb. 1–Mar. 15	Feb. 10–Apr. 1	Feb. 20–Apr. 15	Mar. 1–Apr. 15	Mar. 10–Apr. 15	Mar. 15–May 1	Mar. 25–May 15
Cress, upland	Jan. 1–Feb. 1	Jan. 1–Feb. 15	Jan. 15–Feb. 15	Feb. 1–Mar. 1	Feb. 10–Mar. 15	Feb. 20–Mar. 15	Mar. 1–Apr. 1
Cucumbers	Feb. 15–Mar. 15	Feb. 15–Apr. 1	Feb. 15–Apr. 15	Mar. 1–Apr. 15	Mar. 15–Apr. 15	Apr. 1–May 1	Apr. 10–May 15
Eggplant[1]	Feb. 1–Mar. 1	Feb. 10–Mar. 15	Feb. 20–Apr. 1	Mar. 10–Apr. 15	Mar. 15–Apr. 15	Apr. 1–May 1	Apr. 15–May 15
Endive	Jan. 1–Mar. 1	Jan. 1–Mar. 1	Jan. 15–Mar. 1	Feb. 1–Mar. 1	Feb. 15–Mar. 15	Mar. 1–Apr. 1	Mar. 10–Apr. 10
Fennel, Florence	Jan. 1–Mar. 1	Jan. 1–Mar. 1	Jan. 15–Mar. 1	Feb. 1–Mar. 1	Feb. 15–Mar. 15	Mar. 1–Apr. 1	Mar. 10–Apr. 10
Garlic	(2)	(2)	(2)	(2)	(2)	Feb. 1–Mar. 1	Feb. 10–Mar. 10
Horseradish[1]							Mar. 1–Apr. 1
Kale	Jan. 1–Feb. 1	Jan. 10–Feb. 1	Jan. 20–Feb. 10	Feb. 1–20	Feb. 10–Mar. 1	Feb. 20–Mar. 10	Mar. 1–20
Kohlrabi	Jan. 1–Feb. 1	Jan. 10–Feb. 1	Jan. 20–Feb. 10	Feb. 1–20	Feb. 10–Mar. 1	Feb. 20–Mar. 10	Mar. 1–Apr. 1

Crop	Jan. 30	Feb. 8	Feb. 18	Feb. 28	Mar. 10	Mar. 20	Mar. 30
Leeks	Jan. 1–Feb. 1	Jan. 1–Feb. 1	Jan. 1–Feb. 15	Jan. 15–Feb. 15	Jan. 25–Mar. 1	Feb. 1–Mar. 1	Feb. 15–Mar. 15
Lettuce, head[1]	Jan. 1–Feb. 1	Jan. 1–Feb. 1	Jan. 1–Feb. 1	Jan. 15–Feb. 15	Feb. 1–20	Feb. 15–Mar. 10	Mar. 1–20
Lettuce, leaf	Jan. 1–Feb. 1	Jan. 1–Feb. 1	Jan. 1–Mar. 15	Jan. 1–Mar. 15	Jan. 15–Apr. 1	Feb. 1–Apr. 1	Feb. 15–Apr. 15
Muskmelons	Feb. 15–Mar. 15	Feb. 15–Apr. 1	Feb. 15–Apr. 15	Mar. 1–Apr. 15	Mar. 15–Apr. 15	Apr. 1–May 1	Apr. 10–May 15
Mustard	Jan. 1–Mar. 1	Jan. 1–Mar. 1	Feb. 15–Apr. 15	Feb. 1–Mar. 1	Feb. 10–Mar. 15	Feb. 20–Apr. 1	Mar. 1–Apr. 15
Okra	Feb. 15–Apr. 1	Feb. 15–Apr. 15	Mar. 1–June 1	Mar. 10–June 1	Mar. 20–June 1	Apr. 1–June 15	Apr. 10–June 15
Onions[1]	Jan. 1–15	Jan. 1–15	Jan. 1–15	Jan. 1–Feb. 1	Jan. 15–Feb. 15	Feb. 10–Mar. 10	Feb. 15–Mar. 15
Onions, seed	Jan. 1–15	Jan. 1–15	Jan. 1–15	Jan. 1–Feb. 15	Feb. 1–Mar. 1	Feb. 10–Mar. 10	Feb. 20–Mar. 15
Onions, sets	Jan. 1–15	Jan. 1–15	Jan. 1–15	Jan. 1–Mar. 1	Jan. 15–Mar. 10	Feb. 1–Mar. 20	Feb. 15–Mar. 20
Parsley	Jan. 1–30	Jan. 1–30	Jan. 1–30	Jan. 15–Mar. 1	Feb. 1–Mar. 10	Feb. 15–Mar. 15	Mar. 1–Apr. 1
Parsnips			Jan. 1–Feb. 1	Jan. 15–Feb. 15	Jan. 15–Mar. 1	Feb. 15–Mar. 15	Mar. 1–Apr. 1
Peas, garden	Jan. 1–Feb. 15	Jan. 1–Feb. 15	Jan. 1–Mar. 1	Jan. 15–Mar. 1	Jan. 15–Mar. 15	Feb. 1–Mar. 15	Feb. 10–Mar. 20
Peas, black-eyed	Feb. 15–May 1	Feb. 15–May 15	Mar. 1–June 15	Mar. 10–June 20	Mar. 15–July 1	Apr. 1–July 1	Apr. 15–July 1
Peppers[1]	Feb. 1–Apr. 1	Feb. 15–Apr. 15	Mar. 1–May 1	Mar. 15–May 1	Apr. 1–June 1	Apr. 10–June 1	Apr. 15–June 1
Potatoes	Jan. 1–Feb. 15	Jan. 1–Feb. 15	Jan. 15–Mar. 1	Jan. 15–Mar. 1	Feb. 1–Mar. 1	Feb. 10–Mar. 15	Feb. 20–Mar. 20
Radishes	Jan. 1–Apr. 1	Jan. 1–Apr. 1	Jan. 1–Apr. 1	Jan. 1–Apr. 1	Jan. 1–Apr. 15	Jan. 20–May 1	Feb. 15–May 1
Rhubarb[1]							
Rutabagas				Jan. 1–Feb. 1	Jan. 15–Feb. 15	Jan. 15–Mar. 1	Feb. 1–Mar. 1
Salsify	Jan. 1–Feb. 1	Jan. 10–Feb. 10	Jan. 15–Feb. 20	Jan. 15–Mar. 1	Feb. 1–Mar. 1	Feb. 15–Mar. 1	Mar. 1–15
Shallots	Jan. 1–Feb. 1	Jan. 1–Feb. 10	Jan. 1–Feb. 20	Jan. 1–Mar. 1	Jan. 15–Mar. 1	Feb. 1–Mar. 10	Feb. 15–Mar. 15
Sorrel	Jan. 1–Mar. 1	Jan. 1–Mar. 1	Jan. 15–Mar. 1	Feb. 1–Mar. 10	Feb. 10–Mar. 15	Feb. 10–Mar. 20	Feb. 20–Apr. 1
Soybeans	Mar. 1–June 30	Mar. 1–June 30	Mar. 10–June 30	Mar. 20–June 30	Apr. 10–June 30	Apr. 10–June 30	Apr. 20–June 30
Spinach	Jan. 1–Feb. 15	Jan. 1–Feb. 15	Jan. 1–Mar. 1	Jan. 1–Mar. 1	Jan. 15–Mar. 10	Jan. 15–Mar. 15	Feb. 1–Mar. 20
Spinach, New Zealand	Feb. 1–Apr. 15	Feb. 15–Apr. 15	Mar. 1–Apr. 15	Mar. 15–May 15	Mar. 20–May 15	Apr. 1–May 15	Apr. 10–June 1
Squash, summer	Feb. 1–Apr. 15	Feb. 15–Apr. 15	Mar. 1–Apr. 15	Mar. 15–May 15	Mar. 15–May 1	Apr. 1–May 15	Apr. 10–June 1
Sweet potatoes	Feb. 15–May 15	Mar. 1–May 15	Mar. 20–June 1	Mar. 20–June 1	Apr. 1–June 1	Apr. 10–June 1	Apr. 20–June 1
Tomatoes	Feb. 1–Apr. 1	Feb. 20–Apr. 10	Mar. 1–Apr. 20	Mar. 10–May 1	Mar. 20–May 10	Apr. 1–May 20	Apr. 10–June 1
Turnips	Jan. 1–Mar. 1	Jan. 1–Mar. 1	Jan. 10–Mar. 1	Jan. 20–Mar. 1	Feb. 1–Mar. 1	Feb. 10–Mar. 10	Feb. 20–Mar. 20
Watermelons	Feb. 15–Mar. 15	Feb. 15–Apr. 1	Feb. 15–Apr. 15	Mar. 1–Apr. 15	Mar. 15–Apr. 15	Apr. 1–May 1	Apr. 10–May 15

[1]Plants.

[2]Generally fall-planted.

Source: *Caring for the Garden*, U.S. Department of Agriculture.

Crop	Planting dates for localities in which average date of last freeze is—						
	Apr. 10	Apr. 20	Apr. 30	May 10	May 20	May 30	June 10
Asparagus[1]	Mar. 10–Apr. 10	Mar. 15–Apr. 15	Mar. 20–Apr. 15	Mar. 10–Apr. 30	Apr. 20–May 15	May 1–June 1	May 15–June 1
Beans, lima	Apr. 1–June 30	May 1–June 20	May 15–June 15	May 25–June 15			
Beans, snap	Apr. 10–June 30	Apr. 25–June 30	May 10–June 30	May 10–June 30	May 15–June 30	May 25–June 15	
Beets	Mar. 10–June 1	Mar. 20–June 1	Apr. 1–June 15	Apr. 15–June 15	Apr. 25–June 15	May 1–June 15	May 15–June 15
Broccoli, sprouting[1]	Mar. 15–Apr. 15	Mar. 25–Apr. 20	Apr. 1–May 1	Apr. 15–June 1	May 1–June 15	May 10–June 10	May 20–June 10
Brussels sprouts[1]	Mar. 15–Apr. 15	Mar. 25–Apr. 20	Apr. 1–May 1	Apr. 15–June 1	May 1–June 15	May 10–June 10	May 20–June 10
Cabbage[1]	Mar. 1–Apr. 1	Mar. 10–Apr. 1	Mar. 15–Apr. 10	Apr. 1–May 15	May 1–June 15	May 10–June 15	May 20–June 1
Cabbage, Chinese	([2])	([2])	([2])	Apr. 1–May 15	May 1–June 15	May 10–June 15	May 20–June 1
Carrots	Mar. 10–Apr. 20	Apr. 1–May 15	Apr. 10–June 1	Apr. 20–June 15	May 1–June 1	May 10–June 1	May 20–June 1
Cauliflower[1]	Mar. 1–Mar. 20	Mar. 15–Apr. 20	Apr. 10–May 10	Apr. 15–May 15	May 10–June 15	May 20–June 1	June 1–June 15
Celery and celeriac	Apr. 1–Apr. 20	Apr. 10–May 1	Apr. 15–May 1	Apr. 20–June 15	May 10–June 15	May 20–June 1	June 1–June 15
Chard	Mar. 15–June 15	Apr. 1–June 15	Apr. 15–June 15	Apr. 20–June 15	May 10–June 15	May 20–June 1	June 1–June 15
Chervil and chives	Mar. 1–Apr. 1	Mar. 10–Apr. 10	Mar. 20–Apr. 20	Apr. 1–May 1	Apr. 15–May 15	May 1–June 1	May 15–June 1
Chicory, witloof	June 10–July 1	June 15–July 1	June 15–July 1	June 1–20	June 1–15	June 1–15	June 1–15
Collards[1]	Mar. 1–June 1	Mar. 10–June 1	Apr. 1–June 1	Apr. 15–June 1	May 1–June 1	May 10–June 1	May 20–June 1
Cornsalad	Feb. 1–Apr. 1	Feb. 15–Apr. 15	Mar. 1–May 1	Apr. 1–June 1	Apr. 15–June 1	May 1–June 15	May 15–June 15
Corn, sweet	Apr. 10–June 1	Apr. 25–June 15	May 10–June 15	May 10–June 1	May 15–June 1	May 20–June 1	
Cress, upland	Mar. 10–Apr. 15	Mar. 20–May 1	Apr. 10–May 10	Apr. 20–May 20	May 1–June 1	May 15–June 1	May 15–June 15
Cucumbers	Apr. 20–June 1	May 1–June 15	May 15–June 15	May 20–June 15	June 1–15		
Eggplant[1]	May 1–June 1	May 10–June 1	May 15–June 10	May 20–June 15	June 1–15		
Endive	Mar. 15–Apr. 15	Mar. 25–Apr. 15	Apr. 1–May 1	Apr. 15–May 15	May 1–30	May 1–30	May 15–June 1
Fennel, Florence	Mar. 15–Apr. 15	Mar. 25–Apr. 15	Apr. 1–May 1	Apr. 15–May 15	May 1–30	May 1–30	May 15–June 1
Garlic	Feb. 20–Mar. 20	Mar. 10–Apr. 1	Mar. 15–Apr. 15	Apr. 1–May 1	Apr. 15–May 15	May 1–30	May 15–June 1
Horseradish[1]	Mar. 10–Apr. 10	Mar. 20–Apr. 20	Apr. 1–30	Apr. 15–May 15	Apr. 20–May 20	May 1–30	May 15–June 1
Kale	Mar. 10–Apr. 1	Mar. 20–Apr. 10	Apr. 1–20	Apr. 10–May 1	Apr. 20–May 10	May 1–30	May 15–June 1

Leeks	Mar. 1–Apr. 1	Mar. 15–Apr. 15	Apr. 1–May 1	Apr. 15–May 15	May 1–May 20	May 1–15	May 1–15
Lettuce, head[1]	Mar. 10–Apr. 1	Mar. 20–Apr. 15	Apr. 1–May 1	Apr. 15–May 15	May 1–June 30	May 10–June 30	May 20–June 30
Lettuce, leaf	Mar. 15–May 15	Mar. 20–May 15	Apr. 1–June 1	Apr. 15–June 15	May 1–June 30	May 10–June 30	May 20–June 30
Muskmelons	Apr. 20–June 1	May 1–June 15	May 15–June 15	June 1–June 15			
Mustard	Mar. 10–Apr. 20	Mar. 20–May 1	Apr. 1–May 10	Apr. 15–June 1	May 1–June 30	May 10–June 30	May 20–June 30
Okra	Apr. 20–June 15	May 1–June 1	May 10–June 1	May 20–June 10	June 1–20		
Onions[1]	Mar. 1–Apr. 1	Mar. 15–Apr. 10	Apr. 1–May 1	Apr. 10–May 1	Apr. 20–May 15	May 1–30	May 10–June 10
Onions, seed	Mar. 1–Apr. 1	Mar. 15–Apr. 1	Mar. 15–Apr. 15	Apr. 1–May 1	Apr. 20–May 15	May 1–30	May 10–June 10
Onions, sets	Mar. 1–Apr. 1	Mar. 10–Apr. 1	Mar. 10–Apr. 10	Apr. 10–May 1	Apr. 20–May 15	May 1–30	May 10–June 10
Parsley	Mar. 10–Apr. 10	Mar. 20–Apr. 20	Apr. 1–May 1	Apr. 15–May 15	May 1–20	May 10–June 1	May 20–June 10
Parsnips	Mar. 10–Apr. 10	Mar. 20–Apr. 20	Apr. 1–May 1	Apr. 15–May 15	May 1–20	May 10–June 1	May 20–June 10
Peas, garden	Feb. 20–Mar. 20	Mar. 10–Apr. 10	Mar. 20–May 1	Apr. 1–May 15	Apr. 15–June 1	May 1–June 15	May 10–June 15
Peas, black-eyed	May 1–July 1	May 10–June 15	May 15–June 1				
Peppers[1]	May 1–June 1	May 10–June 1	May 15–June 10	May 20–June 10	May 25–June 15	June 1–15	
Potatoes	Mar. 10–Apr. 1	Mar. 15–Apr. 10	Mar. 20–May 10	Apr. 1–June 1	Apr. 15–June 15	May 1–June 15	May 15–June 1
Radishes	Mar. 1–May 1	Mar. 10–May 10	Mar. 20–May 10	Apr. 1–June 1	Apr. 15–June 15	May 1–June 15	May 15–June 1
Rhubarb[1]	Mar. 1–Apr. 1	Mar. 10–Apr. 10	Mar. 20–Apr. 15	Apr. 1–May 1	Apr. 15–May 10	May 1–20	May 15–June 1
Rutabagas			May 1–June 1	May 1–June 1	May 1–20	May 10–20	May 20–June 1
Salsify	Mar. 10–Apr. 15	Mar. 20–May 1	Apr. 1–May 15	Apr. 15–June 1	May 1–June 1	May 10–June 1	May 20–June 1
Shallots	Mar. 1–Apr. 1	Mar. 15–Apr. 15	Apr. 1–May 1	Apr. 10–May 1	Apr. 20–May 10	May 1–June 1	May 10–June 1
Sorrel	Mar. 1–Apr. 15	Mar. 15–May 1	Apr. 1–May 15	Apr. 15–June 1	May 1–June 1	May 10–June 10	May 20–June 10
Soybeans	May 1–June 30	May 10–June 20	May 15–June 15	May 25–June 10			
Spinach	Feb. 15–Apr. 1	Mar. 1–Apr. 15	Mar. 20–Apr. 20	Apr. 1–June 15	Apr. 10–June 15	Apr. 20–June 15	May 1–June 15
Spinach, New Zealand	Apr. 20–June 1	May 1–June 15	May 1–June 15	May 10–June 15	May 20–June 15	June 1–15	
Squash, summer	Apr. 20–June 1	May 1–June 15	May 1–30	May 10–June 10	May 20–June 15	June 1–20	June 10–20
Sweet potatoes	May 1–June 1	May 10–June 10	May 20–June 10				
Tomatoes	Apr. 20–June 1	May 5–June 10	May 10–June 15	May 15–June 10	May 25–June 15	June 5–20	June 15–30
Turnips	Mar. 1–Apr. 1	Mar. 10–Apr. 1	Mar. 20–May 1	Apr. 1–June 1	Apr. 15–June 1	May 1–June 15	May 15–June 15
Watermelons	Apr. 20–June 1	May 1–June 15	May 15–June 15	June 1–June 15	June 15–July 1		

[1]Plants.

[2]Generally fall-planted.

Source: *Caring for the Garden,* U.S. Department of Agriculture.

Garden planting: latest dates

These are recommended latest dates for getting your seeds or transplants into the ground. If you don't know local frost dates, contact a County Extension Agent.

Crop	Planting dates for localities in which average dates of first freeze is— Aug. 30	Sept. 10	Sept. 20	Sept. 30	Oct. 10	Oct. 20
Asparagus[1]					Oct. 20–Nov. 15	Nov. 1–Dec. 15
Beans, lima				June 1–15	June 1–15	June 15–30
Beans, snap		May 15–June 15	June 1–July 1	June 1–July 10	June 15–July 20	July 1–Aug. 1
Beets	May 15–June 15	May 15–June 15	June 1–July 1	June 1–July 10	June 15–July 25	July 1–Aug. 5
Broccoli, sprouting	May 1–June 1	May 1–June 1	May 1–June 15	June 1–30	June 15–July 15	July 1–Aug. 1
Brussels sprouts	May 1–June 1	May 1–June 1	May 1–June 15	June 1–30	June 15–July 15	July 1–Aug. 1
Cabbage[1]	May 1–June 1	May 1–June 1	May 1–June 15	June 1–July 10	June 1–July 15	July 1–20
Cabbage, Chinese	May 15–June 15	May 15–June 15	June 1–July 1	June 1–July 15	June 15–Aug. 1	July 15–Aug. 15
Carrots	May 15–June 15	May 15–June 15	June 1–July 1	June 1–July 10	June 1–July 20	June 15–Aug. 1
Cauliflower[1]	May 1–June 1	May 1–July 1	May 1–July 1	May 10–July 15	June 1–July 25	July 1–Aug. 5
Celery[1] and celeriac	May 1–June 1	May 15–June 15	May 15–July 1	June 1–July 5	June 1–July 15	June 1–Aug. 1
Chard	May 15–June 15	May 15–July 1	June 1–July 1	June 1–July 5	June 1–July 20	June 1–Aug. 1
Chervil and chives	May 10–June 10	May 1–June 15	May 15–June 15	(2)	(2)	(2)
Chicory, witloof	May 15–June 15	May 15–June 15	May 15–June 15	June 1–July 1	June 1–July 1	June 15–July 15
Collards[1]	May 15–June 15	May 15–June 15	May 15–June 15	June 15–July 15	July 1–Aug. 1	July 15–Aug. 15
Cornsalad	May 15–June 15	May 15–July 1	June 15–Aug. 1	July 15–Sept. 1	Aug. 15–Sept. 15	Sept. 1–Oct. 15
Corn, sweet			June 1–July 1	June 1–July 1	June 1–July 10	June 1–July 20
Cress, upland	May 15–June 15	May 15–July 1	June 15–Aug. 1	July 15–Sept. 1	Aug. 15–Sept. 15	Sept. 1–Oct. 15
Cucumbers			June 1–15	June 1–July 1	June 1–July 1	June 1–July 15
Eggplant[1]				May 20–June 10	May 15–June 15	June 1–July 1
Endive	June 1–July 1	June 1–July 1	June 15–July 15	June 15–Aug. 1	July 1–Aug. 15	July 15–Sept. 1
Fennel, Florence	May 15–June 15	May 15–July 15	June 1–July 1	June 1–July 1	June 15–July 15	June 15–Aug. 1
Garlic	(2)	(2)	(2)	(2)	(2)	(2)
Horseradish[1]	(2)	(2)	(2)	(2)	(2)	(2)
Kale	May 15–June 15	May 15–June 15	June 1–July 1	June 15–July 15	July 1–Aug. 1	July 15–Aug. 15
Kohlrabi	May 15–June 15	June 1–July 1	June 1–July 15	June 15–July 15	July 1–Aug. 1	July 15–Aug. 15

Lettuce, head[1]	May 15–July 1	May 15–July 1	June 1–July 15	June 15–Aug. 1	July 15–Aug. 15	Aug. 1–30
Lettuce, leaf	May 15–July 15	May 15–July 15	June 1–Aug. 1	June 1–Aug. 1	July 15–Sept. 1	July 15–Sept. 1
Muskmelons			May 1–June 15	May 15–June 1	June 1–June 15	June 15–July 20
Mustard	May 15–July 15	May 15–July 15	June 1–Aug. 1	June 15–Aug. 1	July 15–Aug. 15	Aug. 1–Sept. 1
Okra			June 1–20	June 1–July 1	June 1–July 15	June 1–Aug. 1
Onions[1]	May 1–June 10	May 1–June 10	(2)	(2)	(2)	(2)
Onions, seed	May 1–June 1	May 1–June 10	(2)	(2)	(2)	(2)
Onions, sets	May 1–June 1	May 1–June 10	(2)	(2)	(2)	(2)
Parsley	May 15–June 15	May 1–June 15	June 1–July 1	June 1–July 15	June 15–Aug. 1	July 15–Aug. 15
Parsnips	May 15–June 1	May 1–June 15	May 15–June 15	June 1–July 1	June 1–July 10	(2)
Peas, garden	May 10–June 15	May 1–July 1	June 1–July 15	June 1–Aug. 1	(2)	(2)
Peas, black-eye					June 1–July 1	June 1–July 1
Peppers[1]			June 1–June 20	June 1–July 1	June 1–July 1	June 1–July 10
Potatoes	May 15–June 1	May 1–June 15	May 1–June 15	May 1–June 15	May 15–June 15	June 15–July 15
Radishes	May 1–July 15	May 1–Aug. 1	June 1–Aug. 15	July 1–Sept. 1	July 15–Sept. 15	Aug. 1–Oct. 1
Rhubarb[1]	Sept. 1–Oct. 1	Sept. 15–Oct. 15	Sept. 15–Nov. 1	Oct. 1–Nov. 1	Oct. 15–Nov. 15	Oct. 15–Dec. 1
Rutabagas	May 15–June 15	May 1–June 15	June 1–July 1	June 1–July 1	June 15–July 15	July 10–20
Salsify	May 15–June 1	May 10–June 10	May 20–June 20	June 1–20	June 1–July 1	June 1–July 1
Shallots	(2)	(2)	(2)	(2)	(2)	(2)
Sorrel	May 15–June 15	May 1–June 15	June 1–July 1	June 1–July 15	July 1–Aug. 1	July 15–Aug. 15
Soybeans				May 25–June 10	June 1–25	June 1–July 5
Spinach	May 15–July 1	June 1–July 15	June 1–Aug. 1	July 1–Aug. 15	Aug. 1–Sept. 1	Aug. 20–Sept. 10
Spinach, New Zealand				May 15–July 1	June 1–July 15	June 1–Aug. 1
Squash, summer	June 10–20	June 1–20	May 15–July 1	June 1–July 1	June 1–July 15	June 1–July 20
Squash, winter			May 20–June 10	June 1–15	June 1–July 1	June 1–July 1
Sweet potatoes					May 20–June 10	June 1–15
Tomatoes	June 20–30	June 10–20	June 1–20	June 1–20	June 1–20	June 1–July 1
Turnips	May 15–June 15	June 1–July 1	June 1–July 15	June 1–Aug. 1	July 1–Aug. 1	July 15–Aug. 15
Watermelons			May 1–June 15	May 15–June 1	June 1–June 15	June 15–July 20

[1]Plants.

[2]Generally spring-planted.

Source: *Caring for the Garden*, U.S. Department of Agriculture.

Crop	Planting dates for localities in which average date of first freeze is— Oct. 30	Nov. 10	Nov. 20	Nov. 30	Dec. 10	Dec. 20
Asparagus[1]	Nov. 15–Jan. 1	Dec. 1–Jan. 1				
Beans, lima	July 1–Aug. 1	July 1–Aug. 15	July 15–Sept. 1	Aug. 1–Sept. 15	Sept. 1–30	Sept. 1–Oct. 1
Beans, snap	July 1–Aug. 15	July 1–Sept. 1	July 1–Sept. 10	Aug. 15–Sept. 20	Sept. 1–30	Sept. 1–Nov. 1
Beets	Aug. 1–Sept. 1	Aug. 1–Oct. 1	Sept. 1–Dec. 1	Sept. 1–Dec. 15	Sept. 1–Dec. 31	Sept. 1–Dec. 31
Broccoli, sprouting	July 1–Aug. 15	Aug. 1–Sept. 1	Aug. 1–Sept. 15	Aug. 1–Oct. 1	Aug. 1–Nov. 1	Sept. 1–Dec. 31
Brussels sprouts	July 1–Aug. 15	Aug. 1–Sept. 1	Aug. 1–Sept. 15	Aug. 1–Oct. 1	Aug. 1–Nov. 1	Sept. 1–Dec. 31
Cabbage[1]	Aug. 1–Sept. 1	Sept. 1–15	Sept. 1–Dec. 1	Sept. 1–Dec. 31	Sept. 1–Dec. 31	Sept. 1–Dec. 31
Cabbage, Chinese	Aug. 1–Sept. 15	Aug. 15–Oct. 1	Sept. 1–Oct. 15	Sept. 1–Nov. 1	Sept. 1–Nov. 15	Sept. 1–Dec. 1
Carrots	July 1–Aug. 15	Aug. 1–Sept. 1	Sept. 1–Nov. 1	Sept. 15–Dec. 1	Sept. 15–Dec. 1	Sept. 15–Dec. 1
Cauliflower[1]	July 15–Aug. 15	Aug. 1–Sept. 1	Aug. 1–Sept. 15	Aug. 15–Oct. 10	Sept. 1–Oct. 20	Sept. 15–Nov. 1
Celery[1] and celeriac	June 15–Aug. 15	July 1–Aug. 15	July 15–Sept. 1	Aug. 1–Dec. 1	Sept. 1–Dec. 31	Oct. 1–Dec. 31
Chard	June 1–Sept. 10	June 1–Sept. 15	June 1–Oct. 1	June 1–Nov. 1	June 1–Dec. 1	June 1–Dec. 31
Chervil and chives	(2)	(2)	Nov. 1–Dec. 31	Nov. 1–Dec. 31	Nov. 1–Dec. 31	Nov. 1–Dec. 31
Chicory, witloof	July 1–Aug. 10	July 10–Aug. 20	July 20–Sept. 1	Aug. 15–Sept. 30	Aug. 15–Oct. 15	Aug. 15–Oct. 15
Collards[1]	Aug. 1–Sept. 15	Aug. 15–Oct. 1	Aug. 25–Nov. 1	Sept. 1–Dec. 1	Sept. 1–Dec. 31	Sept. 1–Dec. 31
Cornsalad	Sept. 15–Nov. 1	Oct. 1–Dec. 1	Oct. 1–Dec. 1	Oct. 1–Dec. 31	Oct. 1–Dec. 31	Oct. 1–Dec. 31
Corn, sweet	June 1–Aug. 1	June 1–Aug. 15	June 1–Sept. 1			
Cress, upland	Sept. 15–Nov. 1	Oct. 1–Dec. 1	Oct. 1–Dec. 1	Oct. 1–Dec. 31	Oct. 1–Dec. 31	Oct. 1–Dec. 31
Cucumbers	June 1–Aug. 1	June 1–Aug. 15	June 1–Aug. 15	July 15–Sept. 15	Aug. 15–Oct. 1	Aug. 15–Oct. 1
Eggplant[1]	June 1–July 1	June 1–July 15	June 1–Aug. 1	July 1–Sept. 1	Aug. 1–Sept. 30	Aug. 1–Sept. 30
Endive	July 15–Aug. 15	Aug. 1–Sept. 1	Sept. 1–Oct. 1	Sept. 1–Nov. 15	Sept. 1–Dec. 31	Sept. 1–Dec. 31
Fennel, Florence	July 1–Aug. 1	July 15–Aug. 15	Aug. 15–Sept. 15	Sept. 1–Nov. 15	Sept. 1–Dec. 1	Sept. 1–Dec. 1
Garlic	(2)	Aug. 1–Oct. 1	Aug. 15–Oct. 1	Sept. 1–Nov. 15	Sept. 15–Nov. 15	Sept. 15–Nov. 15
Horseradish[1]	(2)	(2)	(2)	(2)	(2)	(2)
Kale	July 15–Sept. 1	Aug. 1–Sept. 15	Aug. 15–Oct. 15	Sept. 1–Dec. 1	Sept. 1–Dec. 31	Sept. 1–Dec. 31
Kohlrabi	Aug. 1–Sept. 1	Aug. 15–Sept. 15	Sept. 1–Oct. 15	Sept. 1–Dec. 1	Sept. 15–Dec. 31	Sept. 1–Dec. 31
Leeks	(2)	(2)	Sept. 1–Nov. 1	Sept. 1–Nov. 1	Sept. 1–Nov. 1	Sept. 15–Nov. 1
Lettuce, head[1]	Aug. 1–Sept. 15	Aug. 15–Oct. 15	Sept. 1–Nov. 1	Sept. 1–Dec. 1	Sept. 15–Dec. 31	Sept. 15–Dec. 31
Lettuce, leaf	Aug. 15–Oct. 1	Aug. 25–Oct. 1	Sept. 1–Nov. 1	Sept. 1–Dec. 1	Sept. 15–Dec. 31	Sept. 15–Dec. 31

Mustard	Aug. 15–Oct. 15	Aug. 15–Nov. 1	Sept. 1–Dec. 1	Sept. 1–Dec. 1	Sept. 1–Dec. 1	Sept. 15–Dec. 1
Okra	June 1–Aug. 10	June 1–Aug. 20	June 1–Sept. 10	June 1–Sept. 20	Aug. 1–Oct. 1	Aug. 1–Oct. 1
Onions[1]		Sept. 1–Oct. 15	Oct. 1–Dec. 31	Oct. 1–Dec. 31	Oct. 1–Dec. 31	Oct. 1–Dec. 31
Onions, seed			Sept. 1–Nov. 1	Sept. 1–Nov. 1	Sept. 1–Nov. 1	Sept. 15–Nov. 1
Onions, sets		Oct. 1–Dec. 1	Nov. 1–Dec. 31	Nov. 1–Dec. 31	Nov. 1–Dec. 31	Nov. 1–Dec. 31
Parsley	Aug. 1–Sept. 15	Sept. 1–Nov. 15	Sept. 1–Dec. 31	Sept. 1–Dec. 31	Sept. 1–Dec. 31	Sept. 1–Dec. 31
Parsnips	([2])	([2])	Aug. 1–Sept. 1	Sept. 1–Nov. 15	Sept. 1–Dec. 1	Sept. 1–Dec. 1
Peas, garden	Aug. 1–Sept. 15	Sept. 1–Nov. 1	Oct. 1–Dec. 1	Oct. 1–Dec. 31	Oct. 1–Dec. 31	Oct. 1–Dec. 31
Peas, black-eye	June 1–Aug. 1	June 15–Aug. 15	July 1–Sept. 1	July 1–Sept. 10	July 1–Sept. 20	July 1–Sept. 20
Peppers[1]	June 1–July 20	June 1–Aug. 1	June 1–Aug. 15	June 15–Sept. 1	Aug. 15–Oct. 1	Aug. 15–Oct. 1
Potatoes	July 20–Aug. 10	July 25–Aug. 20	Aug. 10–Sept. 15	Aug. 1–Sept. 15	Aug. 1–Sept. 15	Aug. 1–Sept. 15
Radishes	Aug. 15–Oct. 15	Sept. 1–Nov. 15	Sept. 1–Dec. 1	Sept. 1–Dec. 31	Aug. 1–Sept. 15	Oct. 1–Dec. 31
Rhubarb[1]	Nov. 1–Dec. 1					
Rutabagas	July 15–Aug. 1	July 15–Aug. 15	Aug. 1–Sept. 1	Sept. 1–Nov. 15	Oct. 1–Nov. 15	Oct. 15–Nov. 15
Salsify	June 1–July 10	June 15–July 20	July 15–Aug. 15	Aug. 15–Sept. 30	Aug. 15–Oct. 15	Sept. 1–Oct. 31
Shallots	([2])	Aug. 1–Oct. 1	Aug. 15–Oct. 1	Aug. 15–Oct. 15	Sept. 15–Nov. 1	Sept. 15–Nov. 1
Sorrel	Aug. 1–Sept. 15	Aug. 15–Oct. 1	Aug. 15–Oct. 15	Sept. 1–Nov. 15	Sept. 1–Dec. 15	Sept. 1–Dec. 31
Soybeans	June 1–July 15	June 1–July 25	June 1–July 30	June 1–July 30	June 1–July 30	June 1–July 30
Spinach	Sept. 1–Oct. 1	Sept. 15–Nov. 1	Oct. 1–Dec. 1	Oct. 1–Dec. 31	Oct. 1–Dec. 31	Oct. 1–Dec. 31
Spinach, New Zealand	June 1–Aug. 1	June 1–Aug. 15	June 1–Aug. 15			
Squash, summer	June 1–Aug. 1	June 1–Aug. 10	June 1–Aug. 20	June 1–Sept. 1	June 1–Sept. 15	June 1–Oct. 1
Squash, winter	June 10–July 10	June 20–July 20	July 1–Aug. 1	July 15–Aug. 15	Aug. 1–Sept. 1	Aug. 1–Sept. 1
Sweet potatoes	June 1–15	June 1–July 1	June 1–July 1	June 1–July 1	June 1–July 1	June 1–July 1
Tomatoes	June 1–July 1	June 1–July 15	June 1–Aug. 1	Aug. 1–Sept. 1	Aug. 15–Oct. 1	Sept. 1–Nov. 1
Turnips	Aug. 1–Sept. 15	Sept. 1–Oct. 15	Sept. 1–Nov. 15	Sept. 1–Nov. 15	Oct. 1–Dec. 1	Oct. 1–Dec. 31
Watermelons	July 1–July 15	July 15–July 30				

[1]Plants.

[2]Generally spring-planted.

Source: *Caring for the Garden,* U.S. Department of Agriculture.

Garden vegetable planting chart

Vegetable	Depth to plant seed (inches)	Number of seeds to sow per foot	Distance between plants (inches)	Distance between rows (inches)	Number of days to germination	Seed Soil Temperature: Needs cool soil	Seed Soil Temperature: Tolerates cool soil	Seed Soil Temperature: Needs warm soil	Weeks needed to grow to transplant size	Days to maturity
Asparagus	1½		18	36	7-21		•		1 year	3 years
Beans, snap bush	1½-2	6-8	2-3	18-30	6-14			•		45-65
Beans, snap pole	1½-2	4-6	4-6	36-48	6-14			•		60-70
Beans, lima bush	1½-2	5-8	3-6	24-30	7-12		•	•		60-80
Beans, lima pole	1½-2	4-5	6-10	30-36	7-12			•		85-90
Beets	½-1	10-15	2	12-18	7-10		•			55-65
Broccoli, sprouting	½	4-6	14-18	24-30	3-10		•		5-7*	60-80T
Brussels Sprouts	½	4-6	12-18	24-30	3-10		•		4-6*	80-90T
Cabbage	½	4-6	12-20	24-30	4-10		•		5-7*	65-95T
Carrots	¼	15-20	1-2	14-24	10-17		•			60-80
Cauliflower	½	4-6	18	24-30	4-10		•		5-7*	55-65T
Celery	⅛	4-6	8	24-30	9-21	•			10-12*	90-120T
Chard, Swiss	1	4-6	4-8	18-24	7-10		•			55-65
Chives	½	4-6	8	10-16	8-12		•			80-90
Collards	¼	4-6	10-15	24-30	4-10		•		4-6*	65-85T
Corn, Sweet	2	4-6	10-14	30-36	6-10			•		60-90
Cress, garden	¼	10-12	2-3	12-16	4-10		•			25-45
Cucumbers	1	4-6	12	48-72	6-10			•	4	55-65
Eggplant	¼-½	2-4	18	36	7-14			•	6-9*	75-95T
Endive	½	4-6	9-12	12-24	5-9		•		4-6	60-90
Fennel, Florence	½	8-12	6	18-24	6-17		•			120
Garlic	1		2-4	12-18	6-10		•			90-sets
Horseradish	Div.		10-18	24			•			6-8 mos.

Kohlrabi	½	8-12	3-4	18-24	3-10		•		4-6	60-70
Leeks	½-1	8-12	2-4	12-18	7-12		•		10-12	80-90T
Lettuce, head	¼-½	4-8	12-14	18-24	4-10	•			3-5	55-80
Lettuce, leaf	¼-½	8-12	4-6	12-18	4-10	•			3-5	45-60
Muskmelons	1	3-6	12	48-72	4-8			•	3-4	75-100
Mustard	½	8-10	2-6	12-18	3-10		•			40-60
Nasturtiums	½-1	4-8	4-10	18-36			•			50-60
Okra	1	4-6	15-18	28-36	7-14			•		50-60
Onions, sets	1-2		2-3	12-24		•				95-120
Onions, plants	2-3		2-3	12-24		•			8	95-120T
Onions, seed	½	10-15	2-3	12-24	7-12	•				100-165
Parsley	¼-½	10-15	3-6	12-20	14-28		•		8	85-90
Parsnips	½	8-12	3-4	16-24	15-25		•			100-120
Peas	2	6-7	2-3	18-30	6-15	•				65-85
Peppers	¼	6-8	18-24	24-36	10-20			•	6-8	60-80T
Potatoes	4	1	12	24-36	8-16		•			90-105
Pumpkins	1-1½	2	30	72-120	6-10			•		70-110
Radishes	½	14-16	1-2	6-12	3-10	•				20-50
Rhubarb	Crown		36	60			•			(**)
Rutabagas	½	4-6	8-12	18-24	3-10		•			80-90
Spinach	½	10-12	2-4	12-14	6-14	•				40-65
Spinach, Malabar	½	4-6	12	12	10		•			70
Spinach, New Zealand	1½	4-6	18	24	5-10		•			70-80
Spinach, Tampala	¼-½	3-4	4-6	24-30			•			21-42
Squash (summer)	1	4-6	16-24	36-60	3-12			•		50-60
Squash (winter)	1	1-2	24-48	72-120	6-10			•		85-120
Sweet potatoes	Plants		12-18	36-48				•		120
Tomatoes	½		18-36	36-60	6-14			•	5-7	55-90T
Turnips	½	12-14	1-3	15-18	3-10	•				45-60
Watermelons	1	3-4	12-16	60	3-12			•		80-100

*Transplants preferred over seed. T=Number of days from setting out transplants; all others are from seeding. (**)=2nd season

Source: The Bruce Company.

Glues: how to choose

Select a glue that has the most qualities you want and the fewest qualities you don't want.

	Bituminous & Mastics	Cyanoacrylate	Epoxy	Hot Melt Glues	Plastic Cements
Ingredients	Tarry chemicals and sticky plastics.	Powerful chemicals.	Powerful chemicals.	Synthetic resins, often phenoxy plastics.	Plastics dissolved in volatile solvents.
Packaging	Cans, caulking tubes.	Small tubes and bottles.	Tubes, cans.	Sticks sized to fit heater.	Generally small tubes.
Form	Paste.	Liquid.	Liquids or pastes mixed at time of application.	Solid. Melts inside the heater compartment.	Liquid.
Strength	Low but adequate for specified jobs.	Very high.	Very high.	Moderate.	Moderate at best.
Flexibility	Moderate but adequate for specified jobs.	High.	Very low.	Low.	Moderate.
Set time	Slow (hours or days).	Few seconds.	Moderate (hours).	Very fast.	Very fast (minutes).
Setting method	Loss of solvents.	Internal chemical reaction.	Internal chemical reactions.	Cooling of glue resins.	Evaporation of solvents.
Travel permitted	Very high.	Low.	High.	Low.	Moderate.
Amount of tack	High.	None (but not vital due to very rapid set time).	Very high for pastes. High to moderate for liquids.	High.	Moderate.
Preferred glue line	Thick ($\frac{1}{16}$–$\frac{1}{8}$″).	Very thin.	Thin for liquids. Thick for pastes.	Thin.	Thin, but can be made thicker by repeated applications.
RESISTANCE TO:					
Moisture	Low except for special formulations.	High.	Very high.	Moderate.	Moderate.
Mold & Mildew	Low except for special formulations.	Very high.	Very high.	Moderate.	High.
Chemicals & solvents	Low.	High.	High.	High.	Low.
Heat	Low.	Very high.	Very high.	Low.	Moderate.
Clamping required?	No.	No.	Very seldom.	No.	Very seldom.
Relative cost	Very low.	Very high.	High.	High.	Low.
Application	Used for sticking floor tile to floor. Also for holding wall panels onto wall.	Repairs on smooth surfaces. Small constructions require fast set time and high strength.	Repairs to wood, glass, tile, pottery, metal, most plastic, leather, fiberglass, etc.	Assembling wood, leather, some plastics, metal, paper, cardboard.	Light repair or construction such as models, textiles, paper.

	Polyvinal Acetate	Resorcinol	Rubber Cement	Silicone Rubber	Urea-Formaldehyde Resins	Urethane
Ingredients	Plastics suspended in watery solvent	Industrial chemicals.	Natural or synthetic rubbers dissolved in	Industrial chemicals.	Industrial chemicals.	Industrial chemicals.

Packaging	Bottles of many sizes.	Bottles. Cans.	Cans. Tubes. Jars.	Tubes. Caulking tubes.	Cans.	Tubes.
Form	Liquid (milky, white).	Liquids; two parts mixed at time of application.	Liquid.	Paste.	Powder that is mixed with water at time of application.	Viscous liquid.
Strength	Moderate.	High.	Low.	High to very high, depending on items bonded.	Moderate.	High.
Flexibility	High.	Moderate.	Very high.	Very high.	Low.	Moderate.
Set time	Moderate (hours).	Slow.	Fast (generally in minutes).	Moderate (hours).	Slow (hours to days).	Moderate (hours).
Setting method	Evaporation of solvent and water.	Internal chemical reactions.	Evaporation of solvents.	Chemical reaction set off by moisture in the air.	Internal chemical reactions.	Evaporation of solvent.
Travel permitted	High.	High.	Very high.	Very high.	Very high.	Very high.
Amount of tack	Moderate.	Moderate.	High.	Very high.	Moderate to low.	High.
Preferred glue line	Thin to moderate.	Thin.	Thin, but specific products can use heavier glue lines.	Thick (⅛″–¼″).	Thin.	Thin to moderate.
RESISTANCE TO:						
Moisture	Moderate.	Excellent.	Fair.	Excellent.	Poor.	Excellent.
Mold & Mildew	High.	Excellent.	Low.	Poor unless label specifies additives are present.	Good.	Excellent.
Chemicals & solvents	Moderate.	Good.	Very low.	Good.	Excellent.	Excellent.
Heat	Moderate.	Excellent.	Low.	Excellent.	Excellent.	Excellent.
Clamping required?	Often, when used for wood projects.	Yes.	No.	No.	Yes.	Seldom.
Relative cost	Low.	Moderate.	Low to moderate.	High.	Moderate.	Moderate.
Application	Excellent for crafts since it dries colorless. Good for paper, textiles, some plastic, wood, photographs, etc. Most nontoxic of popular household adhesives.	Outdoor furniture, boats, toys, etc.	Used to bond flexible materials to other flexible materials or solids such as textiles or plastics to metal, wood, rigid plastic. Also rubber or leather to wood or metal. Can be used as one-shot glue or as contact cement.	Can bond most materials, including glass and metal. Especially good for two solids of different composition subjected to heat, vibration, and similar environmental abuses.	Indoor wood, furniture.	Repairs to wood, glass, tile, pottery, metal, most plastic, leather, fiberglass, etc.

Source: *How to Fix Damn Near Everything*, Peterson

Header sizes to use in framing doors and windows

The header is the horizontal support above a door or window that supports the weight of the wall at that point.

Maximum span (feet)	Header size
3½	Two 2 x 6s
5	Two 2 x 8s
6½	Two 2 x 10s
8·	Two 2 x 12s

Source: *How to Improve Damn Near Everything Around Your Home,* Peterson and Kesselman-Turkel.

Interest on savings and certificates of deposit

In considering how much various savings methods are really worth, you have to compare interest as well as methods of compounding. An account paying 10% that adds interest every month pays more in the long run than an account paying 10% but compounded once a year. Compounding means the interest is added to the principal, and interest is paid on that total amount at the end of the next period.

In this chart, you can see how much $1 will be worth after various periods of time at different interest rates and standard methods of compounding. If you want to calculate interest plus principal for a definite amount, simply multiply the figure given in the chart by the amount with which you started. Example: after 5 years, $150 deposited in an account paying 12% interest, compounded quarterly, will give you $270 in the account (1.80 X $150).

		5 Percent Compounded:			
Monthly		Quarterly		Annually	
Months					
1	1.00				
2	1.01				
3	1.01				
4	1.02				
5	1.02				
6	1.03				
7	1.03				
8	1.03	Quarters			
9	1.04	1	1.01		
10	1.04	2	1.02		
11	1.05	3	1.03		
12	1.05	4	1.05		
Years		Years		Years	
1	1.05	1	1.05	1	1.05
2	1.10	2	1.10	2	1.10
3	1.16	3	1.16	3	1.16
4	1.22	4	1.22	4	1.22
5	1.28	5	1.28	5	1.28
6	1.35	6	1.35	6	1.34
7	1.42	7	1.42	7	1.41
8	1.49	8	1.49	8	1.48
9	1.57	9	1.56	9	1.55
10	1.65	10	1.64	10	1.63

	Monthly		5 Percent Compounded: Quarterly		Annually
Years		Years		Years	
11	1.73	11	1.73	11	1.71
12	1.82	12	1.81	12	1.80
13	1.91	13	1.91	13	1.89
14	2.01	14	2.01	14	1.98
15	2.11	15	2.11	15	2.08
16	2.22	16	2.21	16	2.18
17	2.34	17	2.33	17	2.29
18	2.45	18	2.45	18	2.41
19	2.58	19	2.57	19	2.53
20	2.71	20	2.70	20	2.65

	Monthly		5.5 Percent Compounded: Quarterly		Annually
Months					
1	1.00				
2	1.01				
3	1.01				
4	1.02				
5	1.02				
6	1.03				
7	1.03				
8	1.04	Quarters			
9	1.04	1	1.01		
10	1.05	2	1.03		
11	1.05	3	1.04		
12	1.06	4	1.06		
Years		Years		Years	
1	1.06	1	1.06	1	1.06
2	1.12	2	1.12	2	1.11
3	1.18	3	1.18	3	1.17
4	1.25	4	1.24	4	1.24
5	1.32	5	1.31	5	1.31
6	1.39	6	1.39	6	1.38
7	1.47	7	1.47	7	1.45
8	1.55	8	1.55	8	1.53
9	1.64	9	1.63	9	1.62
10	1.73	10	1.73	10	1.71
11	1.83	11	1.82	11	1.80
12	1.93	12	1.93	12	1.90
13	2.04	13	2.03	13	2.01
14	2.16	14	2.15	14	2.12

5.5 Percent Compounded:

Monthly		Quarterly		Annually	
Years		Years		Years	
15	2.28	15	2.27	15	2.23
16	2.41	16	2.40	16	2.36
17	2.54	17	2.53	17	2.48
18	2.69	18	2.67	18	2.62
19	2.84	19	2.82	19	2.77
20	3.00	20	2.98	20	2.92

6 Percent Compounded:

Monthly		Quarterly		Annually	
Months					
1	1.00				
2	1.01				
3	1.02				
4	1.02				
5	1.03				
6	1.03				
7	1.04				
8	1.04	Quarters			
9	1.05	1	1.02		
10	1.05	2	1.03		
11	1.06	3	1.05		
12	1.06	4	1.06		
Years		Years		Years	
1	1.06	1	1.06	1	1.06
2	1.13	2	1.13	2	1.12
3	1.20	3	1.20	3	1.19
4	1.27	4	1.27	4	1.26
5	1.35	5	1.35	5	1.34
6	1.43	6	1.43	6	1.42
7	1.52	7	1.52	7	1.50
8	1.61	8	1.61	8	1.59
9	1.71	9	1.71	9	1.69
10	1.82	10	1.81	10	1.79
11	1.93	11	1.92	11	1.90
12	2.05	12	2.04	12	2.01
13	2.18	13	2.17	13	2.13
14	2.31	14	2.30	14	2.26
15	2.45	15	2.44	15	2.40
16	2.61	16	2.59	16	2.54
17	2.77	17	2.75	17	2.69
18	2.94	18	2.92	18	2.85

6 Percent Compounded: Monthly		Quarterly		Annually	
Years		Years		Years	
19	3.12	19	3.10	19	3.03
20	3.31	20	3.29	20	3.21

6.5 Percent Compounded: Monthly		Quarterly		Annually	
Months					
1	1.01				
2	1.01				
3	1.02				
4	1.02				
5	1.03				
6	1.03				
7	1.04				
8	1.04	Quarters			
9	1.05	1	1.02		
10	1.06	2	1.03		
11	1.06	3	1.05		
12	1.07	4	1.07		
Years		Years		Years	
1	1.07	1	1.07	1	1.07
2	1.14	2	1.14	2	1.13
3	1.21	3	1.21	3	1.21
4	1.30	4	1.29	4	1.29
5	1.38	5	1.38	5	1.37
6	1.48	6	1.47	6	1.46
7	1.57	7	1.57	7	1.55
8	1.68	8	1.67	8	1.65
9	1.79	9	1.79	9	1.76
10	1.91	10	1.91	10	1.88
11	2.04	11	2.03	11	2.00
12	2.18	12	2.17	12	2.13
13	2.32	13	2.31	13	2.27
14	2.48	14	2.47	14	2.41
15	2.64	15	2.63	15	2.57
16	2.82	16	2.81	16	2.74
17	3.01	17	2.99	17	2.92
18	3.21	18	3.19	18	3.11
19	3.43	19	3.40	19	3.31
20	3.66	20	3.63	20	3.52

7 Percent Compounded: Monthly		Quarterly		Annually	
Months					
1	1.01				
2	1.01				
3	1.02				
4	1.02				
5	1.03				
6	1.04				
7	1.04				
8	1.05	Quarters			
9	1.05	1	1.02		
10	1.06	2	1.04		
11	1.07	3	1.05		
12	1.07	4	1.07		
Years		Years		Years	
1	1.07	1	1.07	1	1.07
2	1.15	2	1.15	2	1.14
3	1.23	3	1.23	3	1.22
4	1.32	4	1.32	4	1.31
5	1.42	5	1.41	5	1.40
6	1.52	6	1.52	6	1.50
7	1.63	7	1.62	7	1.61
8	1.75	8	1.74	8	1.72
9	1.87	9	1.87	9	1.84
10	2.01	10	2.00	10	1.97
11	2.15	11	2.15	11	2.10
12	2.31	12	2.30	12	2.25
13	2.48	13	2.46	13	2.41
14	2.66	14	2.64	14	2.58
15	2.85	15	2.83	15	2.76
16	3.05	16	3.03	16	2.95
17	3.28	17	3.25	17	3.16
18	3.51	18	3.49	18	3.38
19	3.77	19	3.74	19	3.62
20	4.04	20	4.01	20	3.87

7.5 Percent Compounded: Monthly		Quarterly		Annually	
Months					
1	1.01				
2	1.01				
3	1.02				

7.5 Percent Compounded:

Monthly		Quarterly		Annually	
Months					
4	1.03				
5	1.03				
6	1.04				
7	1.04				
8	1.05	Quarters			
9	1.06	1	1.02		
10	1.06	2	1.04		
11	1.07	3	1.06		
12	1.08	4	1.08		
Years		Years		Years	
1	1.08	1	1.08	1	1.07
2	1.16	2	1.16	2	1.16
3	1.25	3	1.25	3	1.24
4	1.35	4	1.35	4	1.34
5	1.45	5	1.45	5	1.44
6	1.57	6	1.56	6	1.54
7	1.68	7	1.68	7	1.66
8	1.82	8	1.81	8	1.78
9	1.96	9	1.95	9	1.92
10	2.11	10	2.10	10	2.06
11	2.28	11	2.26	11	2.22
12	2.45	12	2.44	12	2.38
13	2.64	13	2.63	13	2.56
14	2.85	14	2.83	14	2.75
15	3.07	15	3.05	15	2.96
16	3.31	16	3.28	16	3.18
17	3.56	17	3.54	17	3.42
18	3.84	18	3.81	18	3.68
19	4.14	19	4.10	19	3.95
20	4.46	20	4.42	20	4.25

8 Percent Compounded:

Monthly		Quarterly		Annually	
Months					
1	1.01				
2	1.01				
3	1.02				
4	1.02				
5	1.03				
6	1.04				
7	1.05				

8 Percent Compounded:

Monthly		**Quarterly**		**Annually**	
Months					
8	1.05	Quarters			
9	1.06	1	1.02		
10	1.07	2	1.04		
11	1.08	3	1.06		
12	1.08	4	1.08		
Years		Years		Years	
1	1.08	1	1.08	1	1.08
2	1.17	2	1.17	2	1.17
3	1.27	3	1.27	3	1.26
4	1.38	4	1.37	4	1.36
5	1.49	5	1.49	5	1.47
6	1.61	6	1.61	6	1.59
7	1.75	7	1.74	7	1.71
8	1.89	8	1.88	8	1.85
9	2.05	9	2.04	9	2.00
10	2.22	10	2.21	10	2.16
11	2.40	11	2.39	11	2.33
12	2.60	12	2.59	12	2.52
13	2.82	13	2.80	13	2.72
14	3.05	14	3.03	14	2.94
15	3.31	15	3.28	15	3.17
16	3.58	16	3.55	16	3.42
17	3.88	17	3.84	17	3.70
18	4.20	18	4.16	18	4.00
19	4.55	19	4.50	19	4.31
20	4.93	20	4.87	20	4.66

8.5 Percent Compounded:

Monthly		**Quarterly**		**Annually**	
Months					
1	1.01				
2	1.01				
3	1.02				
4	1.03				
5	1.04				
6	1.04				
7	1.05				
8	1.06	Quarters			
9	1.07	1	1.02		
10	1.07	2	1.04		
11	1.08	3	1.07		
12	1.09	4	1.09		

8.5 Percent Compounded: Monthly		Quarterly		Annually	
Years		Years		Years	
1	1.09	1	1.09	1	1.08
2	1.18	2	1.18	2	1.18
3	1.29	3	1.29	3	1.28
4	1.40	4	1.40	4	1.39
5	1.53	5	1.52	5	1.50
6	1.66	6	1.66	6	1.63
7	1.81	7	1.80	7	1.77
8	1.97	8	1.96	8	1.92
9	2.14	9	2.13	9	2.08
10	2.33	10	2.32	10	2.26
11	2.54	11	2.52	11	2.45
12	2.76	12	2.74	12	2.66
13	3.01	13	2.98	13	2.89
14	3.27	14	3.25	14	3.13
15	3.56	15	3.53	15	3.40
16	3.88	16	3.84	16	3.69
17	4.22	17	4.18	17	4.00
18	4.59	18	4.54	18	4.34
19	5.00	19	4.94	19	4.71
20	5.44	20	5.38	20	5.11

9 Percent Compounded: Monthly		Quarterly		Annually	
Months					
1	1.01				
2	1.02				
3	1.02				
4	1.03				
5	1.04				
6	1.05				
7	1.05				
8	1.06	Quarters			
9	1.07	1	1.02		
10	1.08	2	1.05		
11	1.09	3	1.07		
12	1.09	4	1.09		
Years		Years		Years	
1	1.09	1	1.09	1	1.09
2	1.20	2	1.19	2	1.19
3	1.31	3	1.30	3	1.30
4	1.43	4	1.43	4	1.41

9 Percent Compounded: Monthly		Quarterly		Annually	
Years		Years		Years	
5	1.57	5	1.56	5	1.54
6	1.71	6	1.71	6	1.68
7	1.87	7	1.86	7	1.83
8	2.05	8	2.04	8	1.99
9	2.24	9	2.23	9	2.17
10	2.45	10	2.44	10	2.37
11	2.68	11	2.66	11	2.58
12	2.93	12	2.91	12	2.81
13	3.21	13	3.18	13	3.07
14	3.51	14	3.48	14	3.34
15	3.84	15	3.80	15	3.64
16	4.20	16	4.15	16	3.97
17	4.59	17	4.54	17	4.33
18	5.02	18	4.96	18	4.72
19	5.49	19	5.43	19	5.14
20	6.01	20	5.93	20	5.60

9.5 Percent Compounded: Monthly		Quarterly		Annually	
Months					
1	1.01				
2	1.02				
3	1.02				
4	1.03				
5	1.04				
6	1.05				
7	1.06				
8	1.07	Quarters			
9	1.07	1	1.02		
10	1.08	2	1.05		
11	1.09	3	1.07		
12	1.10	4	1.10		
Years		Years		Years	
1	1.10	1	1.10	1	1.09
2	1.21	2	1.21	2	1.20
3	1.33	3	1.33	3	1.31
4	1.46	4	1.46	4	1.44
5	1.61	5	1.60	5	1.57
6	1.76	6	1.76	6	1.72
7	1.94	7	1.93	7	1.89

9.5 Percent Compounded: Monthly		Quarterly		Annually	
Years		Years		Years	
8	2.13	8	2.12	8	2.07
9	2.34	9	2.33	9	2.26
10	2.58	10	2.56	10	2.48
11	2.83	11	2.81	11	2.71
12	3.11	12	3.09	12	2.97
13	3.42	13	3.39	13	3.25
14	3.76	14	3.72	14	3.56
15	4.13	15	4.09	15	3.90
16	4.54	16	4.49	16	4.27
17	5.00	17	4.93	17	4.68
18	5.49	18	5.42	18	5.12
19	6.04	19	5.95	19	5.61
20	6.64	20	6.54	20	6.14

10 Percent Compounded: Monthly		Quarterly		Annually	
Months					
1	1.01				
2	1.02				
3	1.03				
4	1.03				
5	1.04				
6	1.05				
7	1.06				
8	1.07	Quarters			
9	1.08	1	1.02		
10	1.09	2	1.05		
11	1.10	3	1.07		
12	1.10	4	1.10		
Years		Years		Years	
1	1.10	1	1.10	1	1.10
2	1.22	2	1.22	2	1.21
3	1.35	3	1.34	3	1.33
4	1.49	4	1.48	4	1.46
5	1.65	5	1.64	5	1.61
6	1.82	6	1.81	6	1.77
7	2.01	7	1.99	7	1.95
8	2.22	8	2.20	8	2.14
9	2.45	9	2.43	9	2.36
10	2.71	10	2.68	10	2.59
11	2.99	11	2.96	11	2.85

		10 Percent Compounded:			
Monthly		Quarterly		Annually	
Years		Years		Years	
12	3.30	12	3.27	12	3.14
13	3.65	13	3.61	13	3.45
14	4.03	14	3.99	14	3.80
15	4.45	15	4.40	15	4.18
16	4.92	16	4.86	16	4.59
17	5.43	17	5.36	17	5.05
18	6.00	18	5.92	18	5.56
19	6.63	19	6.53	19	6.12
20	7.33	20	7.21	20	6.73

		11 Percent Compounded:			
Monthly		Quarterly		Annually	
Months					
1	1.01				
2	1.02				
3	1.03				
4	1.04				
5	1.05				
6	1.06				
7	1.07				
8	1.08	Quarters			
9	1.09	1	1.03		
10	1.10	2	1.06		
11	1.11	3	1.08		
12	1.12	4	1.11		
Years		Years		Years	
1	1.12	1	1.11	1	1.11
2	1.24	2	1.24	2	1.23
3	1.39	3	1.38	3	1.37
4	1.55	4	1.54	4	1.52
5	1.73	5	1.72	5	1.69
6	1.93	6	1.92	6	1.87
7	2.15	7	2.14	7	2.08
8	2.40	8	2.38	8	2.30
9	2.68	9	2.66	9	2.56
10	2.99	10	2.96	10	2.84
11	3.33	11	3.30	11	3.15
12	3.72	12	3.68	12	3.50
13	4.15	13	4.10	13	3.88
14	4.63	14	4.57	14	4.31
15	5.17	15	5.09	15	4.78

11 Percent Compounded:

Monthly		Quarterly		Annually	
Years		Years		Years	
16	5.77	16	5.68	16	5.31
17	6.43	17	6.33	17	5.89
18	7.18	18	7.05	18	6.54
19	8.01	19	7.86	19	7.26
20	8.93	20	8.76	20	8.06

12 Percent Compounded:

Monthly		Quarterly		Annually	
Months					
1	1.01				
2	1.02				
3	1.03				
4	1.04				
5	1.05				
6	1.06				
7	1.07				
8	1.08	Quarters			
9	1.09	1	1.03		
10	1.10	2	1.06		
11	1.12	3	1.09		
12	1.13	4	1.13		
Years		Years		Years	
1	1.13	1	1.12	1	1.12
2	1.27	2	1.27	2	1.25
3	1.43	3	1.43	3	1.40
4	1.61	4	1.60	4	1.57
5	1.82	5	1.80	5	1.76
6	2.05	6	2.03	6	1.97
7	2.30	7	2.29	7	2.21
8	2.60	8	2.58	8	2.48
9	2.93	9	2.90	9	2.77
10	3.30	10	3.26	10	3.10
11	3.72	11	3.67	11	3.49
12	4.19	12	4.13	12	3.90
13	4.72	13	4.65	13	4.36
14	5.32	14	5.23	14	4.89
15	6.00	15	5.89	15	5.47
16	6.76	16	6.63	16	6.13
17	7.61	17	7.46	17	6.87
18	8.58	18	8.40	18	7.69
19	9.67	19	9.45	19	8.61
20	10.89	20	10.64	20	9.65

13 Percent Compounded: Monthly		Quarterly		Annually	
Months					
1	1.01				
2	1.02				
3	1.03				
4	1.04				
5	1.06				
6	1.07				
7	1.08				
8	1.09	Quarters			
9	1.10	1	1.03		
10	1.11	2	1.07		
11	1.13	3	1.10		
12	1.14	4	1.14		
Years		Years		Years	
1	1.14	1	1.14	1	1.13
2	1.30	2	1.29	2	1.28
3	1.47	3	1.47	3	1.44
4	1.68	4	1.67	4	1.63
5	1.91	5	1.90	5	1.84
6	2.17	6	2.15	6	2.08
7	2.47	7	2.45	7	2.35
8	2.81	8	2.78	8	2.66
9	3.20	9	3.16	9	3.00
10	3.64	10	3.59	10	3.39
11	4.15	11	4.08	11	3.83
12	4.72	12	4.64	12	4.33
13	5.37	13	5.28	13	4.90
14	6.11	14	6.00	14	5.53
15	6.96	15	6.81	15	6.25
16	7.92	16	7.74	16	7.07
17	9.01	17	8.80	17	7.99
18	10.25	18	10.00	18	9.02
19	11.67	19	11.37	19	10.20
20	13.28	20	12.92	20	11.52

14 Percent Compounded: Monthly		Quarterly		Annually	
Months					
1	1.01				
2	1.02				
3	1.03				

14 Percent Compounded: Monthly		Quarterly		Annually	
Months					
4	1.05				
5	1.06				
6	1.07				
7	1.08				
8	1.10	Quarters			
9	1.11	1	1.03		
10	1.12	2	1.07		
11	1.14	3	1.11		
12	1.15	4	1.15		
Years		Years		Years	
1	1.15	1	1.15	1	1.14
2	1.32	2	1.32	2	1.30
3	1.52	3	1.51	3	1.48
4	1.75	4	1.73	4	1.69
5	2.01	5	1.99	5	1.92
6	2.31	6	2.28	6	2.19
7	2.65	7	2.62	7	2.50
8	3.05	8	3.01	8	2.85
9	3.50	9	3.45	9	3.25
10	4.02	10	3.96	10	3.71
11	4.62	11	4.54	11	4.22
12	5.31	12	5.21	12	4.82
13	6.11	13	5.98	13	5.49
14	7.02	14	6.87	14	6.26
15	8.07	15	7.88	15	7.14
16	9.27	16	9.04	16	8.14
17	10.66	17	10.37	17	9.28
18	12.25	18	11.90	18	10.58
19	14.08	19	13.66	19	12.06
20	16.18	20	15.68	20	13.74

15 Percent Compounded: Monthly		Quarterly		Annually	
Months					
1	1.01				
2	1.03				
3	1.04				
4	1.05				
5	1.06				
6	1.08				
7	1.09				

15 Percent Compounded: Monthly		Quarterly		Annually	
Months					
8	1.10	Quarters			
9	1.12	1	1.04		
10	1.13	2	1.08		
11	1.15	3	1.12		
12	1.16	4	1.16		
Years		Years		Years	
1	1.16	1	1.16	1	1.15
2	1.35	2	1.34	2	1.32
3	1.56	3	1.56	3	1.52
4	1.82	4	1.80	4	1.75
5	2.11	5	2.09	5	2.01
6	2.45	6	2.42	6	2.31
7	2.84	7	2.80	7	2.66
8	3.30	8	3.25	8	3.06
9	3.83	9	3.76	9	3.52
10	4.44	10	4.36	10	4.04
11	5.15	11	5.05	11	4.65
12	5.98	12	5.85	12	5.35
13	6.94	13	6.78	13	6.15
14	8.06	14	7.86	14	7.08
15	9.36	15	9.11	15	8.14
16	10.86	16	10.55	16	9.36
17	12.61	17	12.22	17	10.76
18	14.63	18	14.16	18	12.38
19	16.99	19	16.41	19	14.23
20	19.71	20	19.01	20	16.37

16 Percent Compounded: Monthly		Quarterly		Annually	
Months					
1	1.01				
2	1.02				
3	1.04				
4	1.05				
5	1.07				
6	1.08				
7	1.10				
8	1.11	Quarters			
9	1.13	1	1.04		
10	1.14	2	1.08		
11	1.16	3	1.12		
12	1.17	4	1.17		

16 Percent Compounded:

Monthly		Quarterly		Annually	
Years		Years		Years	
1	1.17	1	1.17	1	1.16
2	1.37	2	1.37	2	1.34
3	1.61	3	1.60	3	1.56
4	1.89	4	1.87	4	1.81
5	2.21	5	2.19	5	2.10
6	2.59	6	2.56	6	2.43
7	3.04	7	3.00	7	2.82
8	3.57	8	3.51	8	3.28
9	4.18	9	4.10	9	3.80
10	4.90	10	4.80	10	4.41
11	5.74	11	5.62	11	5.11
12	6.73	12	6.57	12	5.94
13	7.89	13	7.69	13	6.89
14	9.25	14	8.99	14	7.99
15	10.85	15	10.52	15	9.26
16	12.71	16	12.31	16	10.75
17	14.91	17	14.40	17	12.47
18	17.48	18	16.84	18	14.46
19	20.49	19	19.70	19	16.78
20	24.02	20	23.05	20	19.46

17 Percent Compounded:

Monthly		Quarterly		Annually	
Months					
1	1.01				
2	1.03				
3	1.04				
4	1.06				
5	1.07				
6	1.09				
7	1.10				
8	1.12	Quarters			
9	1.13	1	1.04		
10	1.15	2	1.09		
11	1.17	3	1.13		
12	1.18	4	1.18		
Years		Years		Years	
1	1.18	1	1.18	1	1.17
2	1.40	2	1.39	2	1.37
3	1.66	3	1.65	3	1.60

		17 Percent Compounded:			
Monthly		Quarterly		Annually	
Years		Years		Years	
4	1.96	4	1.95	4	1.87
5	2.32	5	2.30	5	2.19
6	2.75	6	2.71	6	2.56
7	3.26	7	3.21	7	3.00
8	3.86	8	3.79	8	3.51
9	4.57	9	4.47	9	4.11
10	5.41	10	5.28	10	4.80
11	6.40	11	6.24	11	5.62
12	7.58	12	7.37	12	6.58
13	8.97	13	8.71	13	7.70
14	10.62	14	10.28	14	9.00
15	12.58	15	12.15	15	10.53
16	14.89	16	14.35	16	12.33
17	17.63	17	16.95	17	14.42
18	20.87	18	20.02	18	16.88
19	24.71	19	23.65	19	19.75
20	29.26	20	27.93	20	23.10

Interest tables—consumer installment loans

Use these short-term interest tables for consumer loans. You can calculate the amount of monthly payments for cars, jewelry, appliances, etc., or how much total interest you will pay (total finance charge). To calculate interest or monthly payments for financed amounts not shown here, simply add up appropriate amounts within a single vertical column. Example: To find the monthly payments on a loan of $3,100 at 8 percent interest for 2 years, add figures from $3,000 ($136) and $100 ($5) to get $141 monthly payment. (Amounts shown are rounded off to the nearest whole dollar.)

8 Percent Annual Percentage Rate

	1 Year		2 Years		3 Years		4 Years	
Amount Financed	Monthly Payment	Total Finance Charge	Monthly Payment	Total Finance Charge	Monthly Payment	Total Finance Charge	Monthly Payment	Total Finance Charge
$ 100	9	4	5	9	3	13	2	18
500	44	22	23	43	16	64	12	86
1,000	87	44	45	86	31	128	24	172
1,500	130	66	68	128	47	192	37	258
2,000	174	88	90	171	63	256	49	344
2,500	217	110	113	214	78	321	61	430
3,000	261	132	136	257	94	384	73	516
3,500	304	154	158	299	110	448	85	602
4,000	348	176	181	342	125	513	98	688
4,500	391	197	204	385	141	577	110	773
5,000	435	219	226	427	157	640	122	859
5,500	478	241	249	470	172	705	134	945
6,000	522	263	271	513	188	769	146	1,031

8½ Percent Annual Percentage Rate

	1 Year		2 Years		3 Years		4 Years	
Amount Financed	Monthly Payment	Total Finance Charge	Monthly Payment	Total Finance Charge	Monthly Payment	Total Finance Charge	Monthly Payment	Total Finance Charge
$ 100	9	5	5	9	3	14	2	19
500	44	23	23	46	16	68	12	92
1,000	87	47	45	91	32	137	25	183
1,500	131	70	68	137	47	205	37	275
2,000	174	93	91	182	63	273	49	366
2,500	218	117	114	227	79	341	62	458
3,000	262	140	136	273	95	410	74	550

3,500	305	163	159	318	110	478	86	641
4,000	349	187	182	364	126	546	99	733
4,500	392	210	205	409	142	614	111	824
5,000	436	233	227	455	158	682	123	916
5,500	480	257	250	500	174	751	136	1,007
6,000	523	280	273	546	189	819	148	1,099

9 Percent Annual Percentage Rate

	1 Year		**2 Years**		**3 Years**		**4 Years**	
Amount Financed	**Monthly Payment**	**Total Finance Charge**	**Monthly Payment**	**Total Finance Charge**	**Monthly Payment**	**Total Finance Charge**	**Monthly Payment**	**Total Finance Charge**
$ 100	9	5	5	10	3	14	2	20
500	44	25	23	48	16	72	12	98
1,000	87	50	46	97	32	145	25	195
1,500	131	74	69	145	48	217	37	292
2,000	175	99	91	193	64	290	50	389
2,500	219	124	114	241	80	362	62	487
3,000	262	148	137	289	95	434	75	584
3,500	306	183	160	338	111	507	87	681
4,000	350	198	183	386	127	579	100	778
4,500	394	222	206	434	143	652	112	876
5,000	437	247	228	482	159	724	124	973
5,000	481	272	251	530	175	796	137	1,070
6,000	525	297	274	579	191	869	149	1,167

9½ Percent Annual Percentage Rate

	1 Year		**2 Years**		**3 Years**		**4 Years**	
Amount Financed	**Monthly Payment**	**Total Finance Charge**	**Monthly Payment**	**Total Finance Charge**	**Monthly Payment**	**Total Finance Charge**	**Monthly Payment**	**Total Finance Charge**
$ 100	9	5	5	10	3	16	3	21
500	44	26	23	51	16	77	13	103
1,000	88	52	46	102	32	153	25	206
1,500	132	78	69	153	48	230	38	309
2,000	175	104	92	204	64	307	50	412
2,500	219	131	115	255	80	383	63	515
3,000	263	157	138	306	96	460	75	618
3,500	307	183	161	357	112	536	88	721
4,000	351	209	184	408	128	613	101	824
4,500	395	235	207	459	144	689	113	927
5,000	438	261	230	510	160	766	126	1,030
5,500	482	287	253	560	176	843	138	1,133
6,000	526	313	275	612	192	919	151	1,236

10 Percent Annual Percentage Rate

Amount Financed	1 Year Monthly Payment	1 Year Total Finance Charge	2 Years Monthly Payment	2 Years Total Finance Charge	3 Years Monthly Payment	3 Years Total Finance Charge	4 Years Monthly Payment	4 Years Total Finance Charge
$ 100	9	6	5	11	3	16	3	22
500	44	28	23	54	16	81	13	109
1,000	88	55	46	108	32	162	25	218
1,500	132	83	69	161	48	243	38	326
2,000	176	110	92	215	65	323	51	435
2,500	220	137	115	269	81	404	63	544
3,000	264	165	138	323	97	485	76	652
3,500	308	193	162	376	113	566	89	761
4,000	352	220	185	430	129	647	101	870
4,500	396	248	208	484	145	728	114	979
5,000	440	275	231	538	161	808	127	1,087
5,500	484	302	254	591	177	889	140	1,196
6,000	528	330	277	645	194	970	152	1,305

10½ Percent Annual Percentage Rate

Amount Financed	1 Year Monthly Payment	1 Year Total Finance Charge	2 Years Monthly Payment	2 Years Total Finance Charge	3 Years Monthly Payment	3 Years Total Finance Charge	4 Years Monthly Payment	4 Years Total Finance Charge
$ 100	9	6	5	11	3	17	3	23
500	44	29	23	57	16	85	13	115
1,000	88	58	46	113	33	170	26	229
1,500	132	88	70	170	49	260	39	350
2,000	176	116	93	226	65	340	51	458
2,500	221	146	116	284	82	434	64	584
3,000	264	173	139	339	98	510	77	687
3,500	309	204	162	398	114	608	90	818
4,000	353	231	186	452	130	680	102	916
4,500	397	263	208	511	146	781	116	1,051
5,000	441	289	232	565	163	851	128	1,145
5,500	485	321	255	625	179	955	141	1,285
6,000	529	347	278	678	195	1,021	154	1,374

11 Percent Annual Percentage Rate

Amount Financed	1 Year Monthly Payment	1 Year Total Finance Charge	2 Years Monthly Payment	2 Years Total Finance Charge	3 Years Monthly Payment	3 Years Total Finance Charge	4 Years Monthly Payment	4 Years Total Finance Charge
$ 100	9	6	5	12	3	18	3	24
500	44	30	23	59	16	89	13	121
1,000	88	61	47	119	33	179	26	241

1,500	133	91	70	178	49	268	39	361
2,000	177	121	93	237	65	357	52	482
2,500	221	152	117	296	82	447	65	602
3,000	265	182	140	356	98	536	78	722
3,500	309	212	163	415	115	625	90	842
4,000	354	242	186	475	131	715	103	963
4,500	398	273	210	534	147	804	116	1,083
5,000	442	303	233	593	164	893	129	1,203
5,500	486	333	256	652	180	983	142	1,324
6,000	530	363	280	712	196	1,072	155	1,444

11½ Percent Annual Percentage Rate

	1 Year		**2 Years**		**3 Years**		**4 Years**	
Amount Financed	**Monthly Payment**	**Total Finance Charge**	**Monthly Payment**	**Total Finance Charge**	**Monthly Payment**	**Total Finance Charge**	**Monthly Payment**	**Total Finance Charge**
$ 100	9	6	5	13	3	19	3	25
500	44	32	23	62	16	94	13	126
1,000	89	63	47	124	33	187	26	252
1,500	133	97	70	188	50	282	39	378
2,000	177	127	94	249	66	375	52	504
2,500	222	161	117	314	83	470	65	632
3,000	266	190	141	373	99	561	78	757
3,500	310	225	164	440	116	658	91	885
4,000	354	254	187	497	132	749	104	1,009
4,500	399	290	211	565	149	846	117	1,138
5,000	443	317	234	621	165	936	130	1,262
5,500	488	354	258	691	182	1,034	144	1,390
6,000	532	380	281	745	198	1,123	157	1,514

12 Percent Annual Percentage Rate

	1 Year		**2 Years**		**3 Years**		**4 Years**	
Amount Financed	**Monthly Payment**	**Total Finance Charge**	**Monthly Payment**	**Total Finance Charge**	**Monthly Payment**	**Total Finance Charge**	**Monthly Payment**	**Total Finance Charge**
$ 100	9	7	5	13	3	20	3	27
500	44	33	24	65	17	98	13	132
1,000	89	66	47	130	33	196	26	264
1,500	133	99	71	195	50	294	40	396
2,000	178	132	94	260	66	391	53	528
2,500	222	166	118	325	83	489	66	660
3,000	267	199	141	390	100	587	79	792
3,500	311	232	165	454	116	685	92	924
4,000	355	265	188	519	133	783	105	1,056
4,500	400	298	212	584	149	881	119	1,188

12 Percent Annual Percentage Rate

Amount Financed	1 Year Monthly Payment	1 Year Total Finance Charge	2 Years Monthly Payment	2 Years Total Finance Charge	3 Years Monthly Payment	3 Years Total Finance Charge	4 Years Monthly Payment	4 Years Total Finance Charge
5,000	444	331	235	649	166	979	132	1,320
5,500	489	364	259	714	183	1,076	145	1,452
6,000	533	397	282	779	199	1,174	158	1,584

12½ Percent Annual Percentage Rate

Amount Financed	1 Year Monthly Payment	1 Year Total Finance Charge	2 Years Monthly Payment	2 Years Total Finance Charge	3 Years Monthly Payment	3 Years Total Finance Charge	4 Years Monthly Payment	4 Years Total Finance Charge
$ 100	9	7	5	14	3	21	3	28
500	45	35	24	68	17	102	13	138
1,000	89	69	47	135	33	205	27	276
1,500	134	104	71	206	50	309	40	415
2,000	178	138	95	271	67	409	53	552
2,500	223	173	119	344	84	515	67	692
3,000	267	207	142	406	100	613	80	828
3,500	312	242	166	482	117	721	93	967
4,000	356	276	189	542	134	818	106	1,103
4,500	401	311	213	619	151	927	120	1,246
5,000	445	345	237	677	167	1,022	133	1,379
5,500	490	381	261	757	184	1,133	146	1,522
6,000	535	414	284	812	201	1,226	159	1,655

13 Percent Annual Percentage Rate

Amount Financed	1 Year Monthly Payment	1 Year Total Finance Charge	2 Years Monthly Payment	2 Years Total Finance Charge	3 Years Monthly Payment	3 Years Total Finance Charge	4 Years Monthly Payment	4 Years Total Finance Charge
$ 100	9	7	5	14	3	21	3	29
500	45	36	24	71	17	107	13	144
1,000	89	72	48	141	34	213	27	288
1,500	134	109	71	214	51	320	40	437
2,000	179	144	95	282	67	426	54	576
2,500	224	182	119	356	84	533	67	728
3,000	268	216	143	423	101	639	80	864
3,500	313	255	167	499	118	746	94	1,019
4,000	357	287	190	564	135	852	107	1,151
4,500	402	327	214	641	152	959	121	1,310
5,000	447	359	238	705	168	1,065	134	1,439
5,500	492	400	262	783	185	1,173	148	1,602
6,000	536	431	285	846	202	1,278	161	1,727

13½ Percent Annual Percentage Rate

Amount Financed	1 Year Monthly Payment	1 Year Total Finance Charge	2 Years Monthly Payment	2 Years Total Finance Charge	3 Years Monthly Payment	3 Years Total Finance Charge	4 Years Monthly Payment	4 Years Total Finance Charge
$ 100	9	8	5	15	3	22	3	30
500	45	38	24	73	17	111	14	150
1,000	90	75	48	147	34	222	27	300
1,500	134	113	72	221	51	336	41	451
2,000	179	149	96	293	68	444	54	600
2,500	224	188	120	368	85	560	68	752
3,000	269	224	143	440	102	665	81	899
3,500	314	263	167	515	119	784	95	1,053
4,000	358	299	191	587	136	887	108	1,199
4,500	403	338	215	662	153	1,008	122	1,354
5,000	448	373	239	733	170	1,108	135	1,499
5,500	493	414	263	810	187	1,232	149	1,654
6,000	537	448	287	880	204	1,330	162	1,798

14 Percent Annual Percentage Rate

Amount Financed	1 Year Monthly Payment	1 Year Total Finance Charge	2 Years Monthly Payment	2 Years Total Finance Charge	3 Years Monthly Payment	3 Years Total Finance Charge	4 Years Monthly Payment	4 Years Total Finance Charge
$ 100	9	8	5	15	3	23	3	32
500	45	39	24	76	17	115	14	156
1,000	90	77	48	152	34	230	27	312
1,500	135	116	72	232	51	347	41	473
2,000	180	155	96	305	68	461	55	624
2,500	225	194	120	386	86	578	69	788
3,000	269	232	144	457	103	691	82	935
3,500	314	272	168	540	120	809	96	1,103
4,000	359	310	192	609	137	922	109	1,247
4,500	404	349	216	695	154	1,040	123	1,418
5,000	449	387	240	762	171	1,152	137	1,559
5,500	494	427	265	849	188	1,272	151	1,734
6,000	539	465	288	914	205	1,383	164	1,870

14½ Percent Annual Percentage Rate

Amount Financed	1 Year Monthly Payment	1 Year Total Finance Charge	2 Years Monthly Payment	2 Years Total Finance Charge	3 Years Monthly Payment	3 Years Total Finance Charge	4 Years Monthly Payment	4 Years Total Finance Charge
$ 100	9	8	5	16	3	24	3	32
500	45	40	24	79	17	120	14	162
1,000	90	80	48	158	34	239	28	324

14½ Percent Annual Percentage Rate								
	1 Year		2 Years		3 Years		4 Years	
Amount Financed	Monthly Payment	Total Finance Charge	Monthly Payment	Total Finance Charge	Monthly Payment	Total Finance Charge	Monthly Payment	Total Finance Charge
1,500	135	122	72	239	52	363	41	487
2,000	180	161	97	316	69	479	55	648
2,500	225	203	121	398	86	605	69	812
3,000	270	241	145	474	103	718	83	972
3,500	315	284	169	557	121	847	97	1,137
4,000	360	321	193	632	138	957	110	1,295
4,500	405	365	217	716	155	1,089	124	1,462
5,000	450	401	241	790	172	1,196	138	1,619
5,500	496	447	266	876	190	1,331	152	1,786
6,000	540	482	290	948	207	1,435	165	1,943

15 Percent Annual Percentage Rate								
	1 Year		2 Years		3 Years		4 Years	
Amount Financed	Monthly Payment	Total Finance Charge	Monthly Payment	Total Finance Charge	Monthly Payment	Total Finance Charge	Monthly Payment	Total Finance Charge
$ 100	9	8	5	16	3	25	3	34
500	45	42	24	82	17	124	14	168
1,000	90	83	49	164	35	248	28	336
1,500	135	125	73	246	52	374	42	509
2,000	181	166	97	328	69	496	56	672
2,500	226	209	121	410	87	623	70	848
3,000	271	249	145	491	104	744	84	1,008
3,500	316	293	170	574	121	872	98	1,187
4,000	361	332	194	655	139	992	111	1,344
4,500	406	376	218	738	156	1,121	126	1,526
5,000	451	416	242	819	173	1,240	139	1,680
5,500	497	460	267	902	191	1,371	153	1,865
6,000	542	499	291	982	208	1,488	167	2,016

15½ Percent Annual Percentage Rate								
	1 Year		2 Years		3 Years		4 Years	
Amount Financed	Monthly Payment	Total Finance Charge	Monthly Payment	Total Finance Charge	Monthly Payment	Total Finance Charge	Monthly Payment	Total Finance Charge
$ 100	9	9	5	17	4	26	3	35
500	45	43	24	85	17	129	14	174
1,000	91	86	49	170	35	257	28	348
1,500	136	129	73	257	53	390	42	523
2,000	181	172	97	339	70	514	56	696
2,500	226	215	122	428	88	650	70	872
3,000	271	258	146	508	105	771	84	1,044
3,500	317	301	171	599	123	910	98	1,221

15½ Percent Annual Percentage Rate								
	1 Year		2 Years		3 Years		4 Years	
Amount Financed	Monthly Payment	Total Finance Charge	Monthly Payment	Total Finance Charge	Monthly Payment	Total Finance Charge	Monthly Payment	Total Finance Charge
4,000	362	344	195	678	140	1,027	112	1,392
4,500	407	387	220	770	158	1,170	126	1,570
5,000	452	430	244	847	175	1,284	140	1,741
5,500	498	473	268	942	193	1,430	155	1,918
6,000	543	516	292	1,016	209	1,541	169	2,088

16 Percent Annual Percentage Rate								
	1 Year		2 Years		3 Years		4 Years	
Amount Financed	Monthly Payment	Total Finance Charge	Monthly Payment	Total Finance Charge	Monthly Payment	Total Finance Charge	Monthly Payment	Total Finance Charge
$ 100	9	9	5	18	4	27	3	36
500	45	44	24	88	18	133	14	181
1,000	91	89	49	175	35	266	28	361
1,500	136	134	74	264	53	401	43	545
2,000	181	178	98	350	70	532	57	721
2,500	227	224	123	440	88	668	71	908
3,000	272	266	147	525	105	797	85	1,081
3,500	318	314	172	616	123	935	99	1,271
4,000	363	355	196	701	141	1,063	113	1,442
4,500	409	403	221	792	158	1,202	128	1,634
5,000	454	444	245	876	176	1,328	142	1,802
5,500	499	493	270	968	194	1,470	156	1,997
6,000	544	532	294	1,051	211	1,594	170	2,162

16½ Percent Annual Percentage Rate								
	1 Year		2 Years		3 Years		4 Years	
Amount Financed	Monthly Payment	Total Finance Charge	Monthly Payment	Total Finance Charge	Monthly Payment	Total Finance Charge	Monthly Payment	Total Finance Charge
$ 100	9	9	5	18	4	27	3	37
500	46	46	25	90	18	137	14	186
1,000	91	92	49	181	35	274	29	373
1,500	137	138	74	271	53	412	43	559
2,000	182	184	98	362	71	549	57	746
2,500	228	230	123	452	89	686	72	932
3,000	273	276	148	542	106	823	86	1,118
3,500	319	322	172	633	124	960	100	1,305
4,000	364	368	197	723	142	1,098	114	1,491
4,500	410	414	221	814	159	1,235	129	1,678
5,000	455	460	246	904	177	1,372	143	1,864
5,500	501	506	271	994	195	1,509	157	2,050
6,000	546	552	295	1,085	212	1,646	172	2,237

17 Percent Annual Percentage Rate								
	1 Year		2 Years		3 Years		4 Years	
Amount Financed	Monthly Payment	Total Finance Charge	Monthly Payment	Total Finance Charge	Monthly Payment	Total Finance Charge	Monthly Payment	Total Finance Charge
$ 100	9	10	5	19	4	29	3	39
500	46	47	25	94	18	142	14	193
1,000	91	95	49	187	36	284	29	385
1,500	137	143	74	282	54	428	43	581
2,000	182	189	99	373	71	567	58	771
2,500	228	239	124	470	89	713	72	968
3,000	274	283	148	560	107	851	87	1,155
3,500	320	335	173	658	125	998	101	1,355
4,000	365	378	198	746	143	1,134	115	1,541
4,500	411	430	223	846	161	1,283	130	1,742
5,000	456	472	247	933	178	1,418	144	1,925
5,500	502	526	272	1,034	196	1,569	159	2,130
6,000	547	567	297	1,120	214	1,701	173	2,311

17½ Percent Annual Percentage Rate								
	1 Year		2 Years		3 Years		4 Years	
Amount Financed	Monthly Payment	Total Finance Charge	Monthly Payment	Total Finance Charge	Monthly Payment	Total Finance Charge	Monthly Payment	Total Finance Charge
$ 100	9	10	5	19	4	29	3	40
500	46	48	25	96	18	146	15	198
1,000	91	97	50	193	36	292	29	397
1,500	137	145	75	289	54	439	44	595
2,000	183	194	99	386	72	585	58	794
2,500	229	242	124	282	90	731	73	992
3,000	274	290	149	578	108	877	87	1,190
3,500	320	339	174	675	126	1,023	102	,389
4,000	366	387	199	771	144	1,170	116	1,587
4,500	411	436	224	868	162	1,316	131	1,885
5,000	457	484	249	964	180	1,462	146	1,984
5,500	503	532	273	1,060	197	1,608	160	2,182
6,000	548	581	298	1,157	215	1,754	175	2,381

18 Percent Annual Percentage Rate								
	1 Year		2 Years		3 Years		4 Years	
Amount Financed	Monthly Payment	Total Finance Charge	Monthly Payment	Total Finance Charge	Monthly Payment	Total Finance Charge	Monthly Payment	Total Finance Charge
$ 100	9	10	5	20	4	30	3	41
500	46	50	25	99	18	151	15	205
1,000	92	100	50	198	36	302	29	410
1,500	138	151	75	300	54	455	44	617

18 Percent Annual Percentage Rate								
	1 Year		2 Years		3 Years		4 Years	
Amount Financed	Monthly Payment	Total Finance Charge	Monthly Payment	Total Finance Charge	Monthly Payment	Total Finance Charge	Monthly Payment	Total Finance Charge
2,000	183	200	100	396	72	603	59	820
2,500	229	251	125	500	91	758	74	1,028
3,000	275	300	150	595	108	905	88	1,230
3,500	321	351	175	700	127	1,061	103	1,439
4,000	367	401	200	793	145	1,206	118	1,640
4,500	413	452	225	900	163	1,364	132	1,850
5,000	458	501	250	991	181	1,508	147	2,050
5,500	504	552	275	1,100	199	1,667	162	2,262
6,000	550	601	300	1,189	217	1,809	176	2,460

18½ Percent Annual Percentage Rate								
	1 Year		2 Years		3 Years		4 Years	
Amount Financed	Monthly Payment	Total Finance Charge	Monthly Payment	Total Finance Charge	Monthly Payment	Total Finance Charge	Monthly Payment	Total Finance Charge
$ 100	9	10	5	20	4	31	3	42
500	46	51	25	102	18	155	15	210
1,000	92	103	50	205	36	310	30	412
1,500	138	154	75	307	55	466	44	631
2,000	184	206	100	410	73	621	59	842
2,500	230	257	126	512	91	776	74	1,052
3,000	276	308	151	614	109	931	89	1,262
3,500	322	360	176	717	127	1,086	104	1,473
4,000	368	411	201	819	146	1,242	118	1,683
4,500	414	463	226	922	164	1,397	133	1,894
5,000	460	514	251	1,024	182	1,552	148	2,104
5,500	505	565	276	1,126	200	1,707	163	2,314
6,000	551	617	301	1,229	218	1,862	178	2,525

19 Percent Annual Percentage Rate								
	1 Year		2 Years		3 Years		4 Years	
Amount Financed	Monthly Payment	Total Finance Charge	Monthly Payment	Total Finance Charge	Monthly Payment	Total Finance Charge	Monthly Payment	Total Finance Charge
$ 100	9	11	5	21	4	32	3	44
500	46	53	25	105	18	161	15	118
1,000	92	106	50	210	37	321	30	435
1,500	138	160	76	314	55	482	45	653
2,000	184	213	101	419	73	642	60	870
2,500	231	266	126	524	92	803	75	1,088
3,000	277	319	151	629	110	964	90	1,306
3,500	323	372	176	734	128	1,124	105	1,523
4,000	369	426	202	838	147	1,285	120	1,741

	19 Percent Annual Percentage Rate							
	1 Year		2 Years		3 Years		4 Years	
Amount Financed	Monthly Payment	Total Finance Charge	Monthly Payment	Total Finance Charge	Monthly Payment	Total Finance Charge	Monthly Payment	Total Finance Charge
4,500	415	479	227	943	165	1,445	135	1,958
5,000	461	532	252	1,048	184	1,606	150	2,176
5,500	507	585	277	1,153	202	1,766	164	2,393
6,000	553	638	302	1,258	220	1,927	179	2,611

	19½ Percent Annual Percentage Rate							
	1 Year		2 Years		3 Years		4 Years	
Amount Financed	Monthly Payment	Total Finance Charge	Monthly Payment	Total Finance Charge	Monthly Payment	Total Finance Charge	Monthly Payment	Total Finance Charge
$ 100	9	11	5	22	4	33	3	45
500	46	54	25	108	18	164	15	225
1,000	92	109	51	217	37	328	30	450
1,500	139	163	76	325	55	493	45	674
2,000	185	218	101	434	74	657	60	899
2,500	231	272	127	542	92	821	76	1,124
3,000	277	326	152	650	111	985	91	1,349
3,500	323	381	177	759	129	1,149	106	1,574
4,000	370	435	203	867	148	1,314	121	1,798
4,500	416	490	228	976	166	1,478	136	2,023
5,000	462	544	254	1,084	185	1,642	151	2,248
5,500	508	598	279	1,192	203	1,806	166	2,473
6,000	554	653	304	1,301	221	1,970	181	2,698

	20 Percent Annual Percentage Rate							
	1 Year		2 Years		3 Years		4 Years	
Amount Financed	Monthly Payment	Total Finance Charge	Monthly Payment	Total Finance Charge	Monthly Payment	Total Finance Charge	Monthly Payment	Total Finance Charge
$ 100	9	11	6	22	4	34	3	46
500	46	56	25	111	19	170	15	230
1,000	93	111	51	222	37	339	30	459
1,500	139	167	76	332	56	509	46	689
2,000	185	222	102	443	74	678	61	918
2,500	232	278	127	554	93	848	76	1,148
3,000	278	334	153	665	112	1,018	91	1,378
3,500	324	389	178	776	130	1,187	106	1,607
4,000	370	445	204	886	149	1,357	122	1,837
4,500	417	500	229	997	167	1,526	137	2,066
5,000	463	556	255	1,108	186	1,696	152	2,296
5,500	509	612	280	1,219	205	1,866	167	2,526
6,000	556	667	305	1,330	223	2,035	182	2,755

Source: Bureau of Consumer Protection, Federal Trade Commission

Interest tables—long-term loans

Use these long-term interest tables to estimate monthly payments or total interest to be paid (total finance charge) for major purchases such as mobile homes, home improvements, and so on. To calculate finance charge or monthly payments for financed amounts not shown here, simply add up appropriate amounts within a single vertical column. Example: On a loan of $2,100 for 10 years at 10 percent interest, add amounts for $1,000 ($13), another $1,000 ($13), and for $100 ($1) to get a $27 monthly payment. (Since amounts shown are rounded off to the nearest whole dollar, totaled figures may be off by a dollar or two.)

9 Percent Annual Percentage Rate

	8 Years		10 Years		12 Years		15 Years	
Amount Financed	Monthly Payment	Total Finance Charge	Monthly Payment	Total Finance Charge	Monthly Payment	Total Finance Charge	Monthly Payment	Total Finance Charge
$ 100	1	41	1	52	1	64	1	84
1,000	15	407	13	520	11	640	10	827
5,000	73	2,033	63	2,601	57	3,195	51	4,130
10,000	147	4,065	127	5,202	114	6,389	101	8,257
15,000	220	6,097	190	7,802	171	9,582	152	12,385
20,000	293	8,129	253	10,403	228	12,776	203	16,515

9½ Percent Annual Percentage Rate

	8 Years		10 Years		12 Years		15 Years	
Amount Financed	Monthly Payment	Total Finance Charge	Monthly Payment	Total Finance Charge	Monthly Payment	Total Finance Charge	Monthly Payment	Total Finance Charge
$ 100	2	44	1	56	1	68	1	89
1,000	15	432	13	553	12	680	10	881
5,000	75	2,158	65	2,764	58	3,398	52	4,400
10,000	149	4,315	129	5,528	117	6,796	104	8,797
15,000	224	6,472	194	8,292	175	10,194	157	13,195
20,000	298	8,629	259	11,056	233	13,592	209	17,593

10 Percent Annual Percentage Rate

	8 Years		10 Years		12 Years		15 Years	
Amount Financed	Monthly Payment	Total Finance Charge	Monthly Payment	Total Finance Charge	Monthly Payment	Total Finance Charge	Monthly Payment	Total Finance Charge
$ 100	2	46	1	60	1	73	1	94
1,000	15	457	13	586	12	722	11	935
5,000	76	2,284	66	2,930	60	3,605	54	4,673
10,000	152	4,568	132	5,859	120	7,209	107	9,345
15,000	228	6,852	198	8,788	179	10,815	161	14,016
20,000	303	9,135	264	11,717	239	14,419	215	18,687

10½ Percent Annual Percentage Rate								
	8 Years		10 Years		12 Years		15 Years	
Amount Financed	Monthly Payment	Total Finance Charge	Monthly Payment	Total Finance Charge	Monthly Payment	Total Finance Charge	Monthly Payment	Total Finance Charge
$ 100	2	49	1	62	1	77	1	100
1,000	15	483	14	620	12	764	11	991
5,000	77	2,412	67	3,098	61	3,814	55	4,949
10,000	154	4,823	135	6,193	122	7,628	111	9,897
15,000	232	7,235	202	9,289	184	11,443	166	14,846
20,000	309	9,646	270	12,384	245	15,256	221	19,794

11 Percent Annual Percentage Rate								
	8 Years		10 Years		12 Years		15 Years	
Amount Financed	Monthly Payment	Total Finance Charge	Monthly Payment	Total Finance Charge	Monthly Payment	Total Finance Charge	Monthly Payment	Total Finance Charge
$ 100	2	52	1	66	1	81	1	105
1,000	16	508	14	654	13	806	11	1,047
5,000	79	2,541	69	3,266	63	4,026	57	5,229
10,000	157	5,081	138	6,531	125	8,052	114	10,459
15,000	236	7,620	207	9,796	188	12,078	170	15,688
20,000	314	10,160	276	13,061	251	16,104	227	20,918

11½ Percent Annual Percentage Rate								
	8 Years		10 Years		12 Years		15 Years	
Amount Financed	Monthly Payment	Total Finance Charge	Monthly Payment	Total Finance Charge	Monthly Payment	Total Finance Charge	Monthly Payment	Total Finance Charge
$ 100	2	54	1	69	1	86	1	111
1,000	16	534	14	687	13	849	12	1,104
5,000	80	2,670	70	3,436	64	4,240	58	5,514
10,000	160	5,341	141	6,872	128	8,481	117	11,028
15,000	240	8,011	211	10,308	193	12,720	175	16,541
20,000	320	10,681	281	13,744	257	16,960	234	22,055

12 Percent Annual Percentage Rate								
	8 Years		10 Years		12 Years		15 Years	
Amount Financed	Monthly Payment	Total Finance Charge	Monthly Payment	Total Finance Charge	Monthly Payment	Total Finance Charge	Monthly Payment	Total Finance Charge
$ 100	2	56	1	73	1	90	1	118
1,000	16	561	14	722	13	892	12	1,162
5,000	81	2,802	72	3,609	66	4,458	60	5,802
10,000	163	5,603	143	7,218	131	8,914	120	11,604
15,000	244	8,405	215	10,825	197	13,371	180	17,405
20,000	325	11,206	287	14,434	263	17,827	240	23,207

12½ Percent Annual Percentage Rate								
	8 Years		10 Years		12 Years		15 Years	
Amount Financed	Monthly Payment	Total Finance Charge	Monthly Payment	Total Finance Charge	Monthly Payment	Total Finance Charge	Monthly Payment	Total Finance Charge
$ 100	2	59	1	76	1	94	1	123
1,000	17	587	15	757	13	936	12	1,219
5,000	83	2,934	73	3,783	67	4,677	62	6,093
10,000	165	5,868	146	7,566	134	9,352	123	12,187
15,000	248	8,802	220	11,348	202	14,028	185	18,278
20,000	331	11,736	293	15,131	269	18,704	247	24,372

13 Percent Annual Percentage Rate								
	8 Years		10 Years		12 Years		15 Years	
Amount Financed	Monthly Payment	Total Finance Charge	Monthly Payment	Total Finance Charge	Monthly Payment	Total Finance Charge	Monthly Payment	Total Finance Charge
$ 100	2	62	2	80	1	99	1	129
1,000	17	614	15	793	14	980	13	1,279
5,000	84	3,068	75	3,959	69	4,899	63	6,389
10,000	168	6,136	149	7,918	137	9,796	127	12,775
15,000	252	9,203	224	11,876	206	14,693	190	19,162
20,000	336	12,270	299	15,836	275	19,590	253	25,549

13½ Percent Annual Percentage Rate

Amount Financed	8 Years Monthly Payment	8 Years Total Finance Charge	10 Years Monthly Payment	10 Years Total Finance Charge	12 Years Monthly Payment	12 Years Total Finance Charge	15 Years Monthly Payment	15 Years Total Finance Charge
$ 100	2	64	2	84	1	103	1	134
1,000	17	641	15	828	14	1,025	13	1,338
5,000	85	3,203	76	4,137	70	5,122	65	6,686
10,000	171	6,405	152	8,274	141	10,244	130	13,371
15,000	256	9,608	228	12,410	211	15,364	195	20,055
20,000	342	12,810	305	16,546	281	20,486	260	26,741

14 Percent Annual Percentage Rate

Amount Financed	8 Years Monthly Payment	8 Years Total Finance Charge	10 Years Monthly Payment	10 Years Total Finance Charge	12 Years Monthly Payment	12 Years Total Finance Charge	15 Years Monthly Payment	15 Years Total Finance Charge
$ 100	2	67	2	87	1	107	1	141
1,000	17	668	16	864	14	1,071	13	1,398
5,000	87	3,339	78	4,317	72	5,348	67	6,986
10,000	174	6,677	155	8,632	144	10,696	133	13,972
15,000	261	10,016	233	12,948	216	16,042	200	20,959
20,000	347	13,354	311	17,265	287	21,390	266	27,943

14½ Percent Annual Percentage Rate

Amount Financed	8 Years Monthly Payment	8 Years Total Finance Charge	10 Years Monthly Payment	10 Years Total Finance Charge	12 Years Monthly Payment	12 Years Total Finance Charge	15 Years Monthly Payment	15 Years Total Finance Charge
$ 100	2	70	2	91	1	112	1	147
1,000	18	695	16	900	15	1,115	14	1,459
5,000	88	3,476	79	4,498	73	5,577	68	7,290
10,000	177	6,952	158	8,995	147	11,152	137	14,581
15,000	265	10,427	237	13,493	220	16,728	205	21,869
20,000	353	13,902	317	17,990	294	22,303	273	29,160

15 Percent Annual Percentage Rate								
	8 Years		10 Years		12 Years		15 Years	
Amount Financed	Monthly Payment	Total Finance Charge	Monthly Payment	Total Finance Charge	Monthly Payment	Total Finance Charge	Monthly Payment	Total Finance Charge
$ 100	2	73	2	94	1	117	1	152
1,000	18	723	16	937	15	1,161	14	1,520
5,000	90	3,614	81	4,680	75	5,807	70	7,596
10,000	179	7,228	161	9,361	150	11,613	140	15,193
15,000	269	10,842	242	14,041	225	17,420	210	22,789
20,000	359	14,455	323	18,720	300	23,226	280	30,386

15½ Percent Annual Percentage Rate								
	8 Years		10 Years		12 Years		15 Years	
Amount Financed	Monthly Payment	Total Finance Charge	Monthly Payment	Total Finance Charge	Monthly Payment	Total Finance Charge	Monthly Payment	Total Finance Charge
$ 100	2	76	2	98	2	122	1	159
1,000	18	751	16	974	15	1,209	14	1,581
5,000	91	3,753	82	4,865	77	6,040	72	7,906
10,000	182	7,507	164	9,730	153	12,080	143	15,812
15,000	274	11,260	247	14,594	230	18,119	215	23,718
20,000	365	15,013	329	19,460	307	24,158	287	31,624

16 Percent Annual Percentage Rate								
	8 Years		10 Years		12 Years		15 Years	
Amount Financed	Monthly Payment	Total Finance Charge	Monthly Payment	Total Finance Charge	Monthly Payment	Total Finance Charge	Monthly Payment	Total Finance Charge
$ 100	2	79	2	102	2	126	1	165
1,000	19	779	17	1,011	16	1,255	15	1,644
5,000	93	3,894	84	5,051	78	6,275	73	8,219
10,000	185	7,788	168	10,102	157	12,549	147	16,438
15,000	278	11,682	251	15,152	235	18,823	220	24,656
20,000	371	15,576	335	20,204	313	25,096	294	32,875

Source: Bureau of Consumer Protection, Federal Trade Commission.

Interest tables—mortgages: amount of monthly payment for each $1,000 of mortgage principal

Use these tables to calculate either the total amount of interest you will pay over the lifetime of your mortgage, or the monthly payments. (Numbers have been rounded off to the nearest penny.)

Example A: To find the monthly payment on a $120,000 mortgage for 30 years at 11 percent, locate the intersection of the columns for 30 years and 11 percent, and multiply that figure ($9.53 in this example) by 120 ($120,000 divided by $1,000).

Example B: To find how much total interest you'd pay over the lifetime of the mortgage in Example A, multiply your answer (the monthly payment of $1,143.60) by the number of months (360) and subtract your principal ($120,000) from the result.

	Years						
Rate (%)	**10**	**15**	**20**	**25**	**30**	**35**	**40**
9	$12.67	$10.15	$ 9.00	$ 8.40	$ 8.05	$ 7.84	$ 7.72
9½	12.94	10.45	9.33	8.74	8.41	8.22	8.11
10	13.22	10.75	9.66	9.09	8.78	8.60	8.50
10½	13.50	11.06	9.99	9.45	9.15	8.99	8.89
11	13.78	11.37	10.33	9.81	9.53	9.37	9.29
11½	14.06	11.69	10.67	10.17	9.91	9.77	9.69
12	14.35	12.01	11.02	10.54	10.29	10.16	10.09
12½	14.64	12.33	11.37	10.91	10.68	10.56	10.49
13	14.94	12.66	11.72	11.28	11.07	10.96	10.90
13½	15.23	12.99	12.08	11.66	11.46	11.36	11.31
14	15.53	13.32	12.44	12.04	11.85	11.76	11.72
14½	15.83	13.66	12.80	12.43	12.25	12.17	12.13
15	16.14	14.00	13.17	12.81	12.65	12.57	12.54
15½	16.45	14.34	13.54	13.20	13.05	12.98	12.95
16	16.76	14.69	13.92	13.59	13.45	13.39	13.36
16½	17.07	15.04	14.29	13.99	13.86	13.80	13.77
17	17.38	15.40	14.67	14.38	14.26	14.21	14.19
17½	17.70	15.75	15.05	14.78	14.67	14.62	14.60
18	18.02	16.11	15.44	15.18	15.08	15.03	15.02
18½	18.35	16.47	15.82	15.58	15.48	15.45	15.43
19	18.67	16.83	16.21	15.98	15.89	15.86	15.85
19½	19.00	17.20	16.60	16.39	16.30	16.27	16.26

Rate (%)	Years 10	15	20	25	30	35	40
20	19.33	17.57	16.99	16.79	16.72	16.69	16.68
20½	19.66	17.94	17.39	17.20	17.13	17.10	17.09
21	20.00	18.31	17.78	17.60	17.54	17.52	17.51
21½	20.34	18.69	18.18	18.01	17.95	17.93	17.93
22	20.67	19.06	18.58	18.42	18.36	18.35	18.34
22½	21.02	19.44	18.97	18.83	18.78	18.76	18.76
23	21.36	19.82	19.38	19.24	19.19	19.18	19.17
23½	21.71	20.20	19.78	19.65	19.61	19.59	19.59
24	22.05	20.59	20.18	20.06	20.02	20.01	20.01

Source: Adapted from Publication No. 522, *Basic Payment Tables*, of Financial Publishing Company.

Lumber quality ratings

In order to get the best buy in lumber, you have to measure your needs against the lumber's cost and properties. Pick those properties you need most and determine which species gives them at the lowest price.

1 = highest ranking in the given property
3 = lowest ranking in the given property

	Dry weight	Bending strength	Stiffness	Hardness	Workability	Nail holding	Paint holding	Freedom from shrinking	Freedom from warping	Free of pitch	Decay resistant
Douglas fir	1	1	1	1	2	1	3	2	2	2	2
Hemlock fir	2	2	2	2	2	2	3	2	2	1	2
Englemann spruce/ lodgepole pine	3	3	3	3	2	3	3	2	2	1	3
Southern pine	1	1	1	1	2	1	3	2	2	3	2
Idaho white pine	3	3	3	3	1	3	1	2	1	1	3
Canada spruce/pine/fir	3	2	2	3	2	3	3	2	2	1	3
Western cedar	3	3	3	3	1	3	1	1	1	1	1
California redwood	3	2	2	2	1	2	1	1	1	1	1

Source: University of Wisconsin Extension.

Lumber sizes: nominal vs. actual

Nominal sizes used by the lumber industry do not match the exact sizes of the boards they describe. This chart compares trade designations (nominal size) with actual (dressed) sizes.

	Thickness		Face Width	
Grade	Nominal (Inches)	Minimum Size, Dressed (Inches)	Nominal (Inches)	Minimum Size, Dressed (Inches)
	3/8	5/16	2	1-1/2
	1/2	7/16	3	2-1/2
	5/8	9/16	4	3-1/2
	3/4	5/8	5	4-1/2

"Select" or	1	3/4		6	5-1/2	
"Finish"	1-1/4	1		7	6-1/2	
(19 percent	1-1/2	1-1/4		8	7-1/4	
moisture	1-3/4	1-3/8		9	8-1/4	
content)	2	1-1/2		10	9-1/4	
	2-1/2	2		11	10-1/4	
	3	2-1/2		12	11-1/4	
	3-1/2	3		14	13-1/4	
	4	3-1/2		16	15-1/4	
		Dry Inches	**Green Inches**		**Dry Inches**	**Green Inches**
				2	1-1/2	1-9/16
				3	2-1/2	2-9/16
				4	3-1/2	3-9/16
				5	4-1/2	4-5/8
	1	3/4	25/32	6	5-1/2	5-5/8
				7	6-1/2	6-5/8
"Common"	1-1/4	1	1-1/32	8	7-1/4	7-1/2
				9	8-1/4	8-1/2
	1-1/2	1-1/4	1-9/32	10	9-1/4	9-1/2
				11	10-1/4	10-1/2
				12	11-1/4	11-1/2
				14	13-1/4	13-1/2
				16	15-1/4	15-1/2
				2	1-1/2	1-9/16
				3	2-1/2	2-9/16
				4	3-1/2	3-9/16
	2	1-1/2	1-9/16	5	4-1/2	4-5/8
"Construction"	2-1/2	2	2-1/16	6	5-1/2	5-5/8
	3	2-1/2	2-9/16	8	7-1/4	7-1/2
	3-1/2	3	3-1/16	10	9-1/4	9-1/2
				12	11-1/4	11-1/2
				14	13-1/4	13-1/2
				16	15-1/4	15-1/2
				2	1-1/2	1-9/16
				3	2-1/2	2-9/16
				4	3-1/2	3-9/16
				5	4-1/2	4-5/8
"Construction"	4	3-1/2	3-9/16	6	5-1/2	5-5/8
	4-1/2	4	4-1/16	8	7-1/4	7-1/2
				10	9-1/4	9-1/2
				12	11-1/4	11-1/2
				14		13-1/2
				16		15-1/2
Timbers	5 & Thicker		1/2 Off	5 & Wider		1/2 Off

Source: *Yearbook,* U.S. Department of Agriculture, 1974.

Meat storage periods

To maintain good quality and food safety, use meats before these storage periods have elapsed.

Kind of meat	In a refrigerator 35° F. to 40° F. (Days)	In a freezer at 0° F. or below (Months)
Fresh		
chops, steaks, cutlets	3–5	3–4
ground, stew meat	1–2	3
roasts		
lamb, beef	3–5	6–12
pork, veal	3–5	4–8
variety	1–2	3–4
sausage	1–2	1–2
Processed and cured meat		
bacon, ham, corned beef	7–14	2 or less
bologna, luncheon meat	3–5	—
Cooked meat	1–2	3

Source: *Handbook of Food Preparation,* American Home Economics Association.

Medical specialists' specialties

Specialist	What he or she treats
Allergist	Allergies
Cardiologist	Heart problems
Dermatologist	Skin disorders
Family Practitioner	General medical problems
Gastroenterologist	Diseases of the digestive system and liver
Gynecologist	Female disorders
Hematologist	Blood disorders
Internist	Internal disorders (stomach, abdomen, chest)
Nephrologist	Kidney disorders
Neurologist	Nervous system disorders
Obstetrician	Prenatal care, delivery
Ophthalmologist	Eye diseases
Optometrist	Vision disorders
Pediatrician	Children's growth and diseases
Psychiatrist	Mental and emotional disorders
Urologist	Urinary tract disorders

Source: *Medical Guide & Glosssary,* Indochinese Language Resource Center.

Medicines available over the counter

Symptom	Ingredient to look for	Some brand names
Allergy	chlorpheniramine	Chlor-Trimetron
Cold Congestion	pseudophedrine	Sudafed
Constipation	psyllium hydrophilic mucilloid	Metamucil
Cough	glyceryl guaiacolate	Robitussin 2 G
Diarrhea	kaolin	Kaopectate
Eye irritation	methylcellulose drops	Tearisol Visculose
Fever	aspirin acetaminophen	Bayer Datril
Headache	aspirin acetaminophen	Bayer Datril
Itching	calamine	Calamine Lotion Caladryl Lotion
Motion sickness	dimenhydrinate	Dramamine
Nasal congestion	phenylephrine	Neo-Synephrine
Nausea	phosphorated carbohydrate solution dimenhydrinate	Emetrol Dramamine
Pain	aspirin acetaminophen	SL Certified, Bayer SL Certified, Datril
Poisoning	ipecac	Syrup of Ipecac
Skin fungus (Athlete's foot)	tolnaftate	Tinactin Desenex
Stomach ache	magnesium hydroxide aluminum hydroxide	Maalox Gelusil Liquid
Wounds	3 percent hydrogen peroxide	Hydrogen Peroxide

Source: *Medical Guide & Glossary,* Indochinese Language Resource Center.

Metric equivalents for everyday use

If you don't need precision, only close approximations, these metric values are very useful.

Basic units	
Meter:	a little longer than a yard (about 1.1 yards)
Liter:	a little larger than a quart (about 1.06 quarts)
Gram:	a little more than the weight of a paper clip
Other commonly used units	
Millimeter:	0.001 meter—diameter of paper clip wire
Centimeter:	0.01 meter—a little more than the width of a paper clip (about 0.4 inch)
Kilometer:	1,000 meters—somewhat longer than ½ mile (about 0.6 mile)
Kilogram:	1,000 grams—a little more than 2 pounds (about 2.2 pounds)
Milliliter:	0.001 liter—five of them make a teaspoon

Source: National Bureau of Standards.

Metric system memorizer

Since all metric units are multiples of 10 when compared to larger or smaller units, it is possible to use metrics simply by memorizing the six basic prefixes and the three basic measurements: liter for volume, gram for weight, meter for length. The prefixes follow:

Prefix	Abbreviation	Multiplier	
kilo	k	thousand	1000.
hecto	h	hundred	100.
deka	da	ten	10.
(none)			1.
deci	d	one-tenth	.1
centi	c	one-hundredth	.01
milli	m	one-thousandth	.001

Nail sizes and quantities per pound

The *d* symbol used below is an old English term for the size of nails, still in common use today. The *d* stands for *penny,* so read *6d* as *6 penny.*

Size code	Length (inches)	Approximate number per pound Common		
		Common	Finishing	Shingle
2d	1	830		
3d	1¼	528		429
4d	1½	316	584	274
5d	1¾	271	500	235
6d	2	168	309	
8d	2½	106	189	
10d	3	69	121	
12d	3¼	63		
16d	3½	49	90	
20d	4	31	62	
30d	4½	24		
40d	5	18		
50d	5½	14		
60d	6	11		

Numbers' conversion formulas

Multiply	By	To Obtain
centimeters (cm)	0.0328	feet
centimeters	0.3937	inches
cubic centimeters (cc)	0.06102	cubic inches
cubic inches (cu in)	16.387	cubic centimeters
foot-pounds	0.13826	kilogram meters
feet	30.48	centimeters
feet	0.3048	meters
feet	304.8	millimeters
gallons, Imperial (gal)	0.1605	cubic feet
gallons, Imperial	1.201	gallons, U.S.
gallons, Imperial	4.546	liters
gallons, U.S. (gal)	0.8327	gallons, Imperial
gallons, U.S.	231	cubic inches
gallons, U.S.	3.785	liters
grams (gm)	0.03527	ounces
inches	2.54	centimeters
inches	25.4	millimeters
kilograms (kg)	2.205	pounds
kilogram meters (kg/m)	7.233	foot-pounds
kilograms per square centimeter (kg/cc^2)	14.223	pounds per square inch
kilometers (km)	0.6214	miles
kilometers	3280.7	feet
liters (l)	0.22	gallons (Imperial)
liters	0.2642	gallons (U.S.)
liters	0.03531	cubic feet
liters	61.022	cubic inches
meters (m)	3.281	feet
meters	39.37	inches
meters	1.094	yards
miles (mi)	1.609	kilometers
millimeters (mm)	0.03937	inches
pounds (lb)	453.6	grams
pounds	0.4536	kilograms
pounds per square inch (psi)	0.07031	kilograms per square centimeter
square centimeters	0.155	square inches
square inches	6.452	square centimeters
yards (yd)	0.9144	meters

Numbers converted from inches into decimals into millimeters

Fraction of inch	Decimal inches	Milli-meters
	0.0004	0.01
	0.0008	0.02
	0.0012	0.03
	0.0016	0.04
	0.0020	0.05
	0.0024	0.06
	0.0028	0.07
	0.0031	0.08
	0.0035	0.09
	0.0039	0.10
1/128	0.0079	0.20
	0.0118	0.30
1/64	0.0156	0.40
	0.0197	0.50
	0.0236	0.60
	0.0276	0.70
1/32	0.0313	0.79
	0.0315	0.80
	0.0354	0.90
	0.0393	1.00
3/64	0.0469	1.19
	0.0492	1.25
	0.0590	1.50
1/16	0.0625	1.59
	0.0689	1.75
5/64	0.0781	1.98
	0.0787	2.00
3/32	0.0938	2.38
	0.0984	2.50
	0.1000	2.54
7/64	0.1094	2.78
	0.1181	3.00
1/8	0.1250	3.18
	0.1378	3.50
9/64	0.1406	3.57
	0.1500	3.81
5/32	0.1562	3.97
	0.1574	4.00

Fraction of inch	Decimal inches	Millimeters
11/64	0.1719	4.37
	0.1772	4.50
3/16	0.1875	4.76
	0.1968	5.00
	0.2000	5.08
13/64	0.2031	5.16
	0.2165	5.50
7/32	0.2188	5.56
15/64	0.2344	5.95
	0.2362	6.00
1/4	0.2500	6.35
	0.2559	6.50
17/64	0.2656	6.75
	0.2756	7.00
9/32	0.2812	7.14
19/64	0.2969	7.54
	0.3000	7.62
5/16	0.3125	7.94
	0.3150	8.00
21/64	0.3281	8.33
11/32	0.3438	8.73
	0.3500	8.89
	0.3543	9.00
23/64	0.3594	9.13
	0.3740	9.50
3/8	0.3750	9.52
25/64	0.3906	9.92
	0.3937	10.00
	0.4000	10.16
13/32	0.4062	10.32
	0.4134	10.50
27/64	0.4219	10.72
	0.4331	11.00
7/16	0.4375	11.11
	0.4500	11.43
29/64	0.4531	11.51
15/32	0.4687	11.91
	0.4724	12.00
31/64	0.4844	12.30
	0.4921	12.50
1/2	0.5000	12.70
	0.5118	13.00

Fraction of inch	Decimal inches	Milli-meters
33/64	0.5156	13.10
17/32	0.5312	13.49
	0.5315	13.50
35/64	0.5469	13.89
	0.5500	13.97
	0.5512	14.00
9/16	0.5625	14.29
37/64	0.5781	14.68
	0.5906	15.00
19/32	0.5937	15.08
	0.6000	15.24
39/64	0.6094	15.48
	0.6102	15.50
5/8	0.6250	15.88
	0.6299	16.00
41/64	0.6426	16.27
	0.6500	16.51
21/32	0.6562	16.67
	0.6693	17.00
43/64	0.6719	17.07
11/16	0.6875	17.46
	0.6900	17.50
	0.7000	17.78
45/64	0.7031	17.86
	0.7087	18.00
23/32	0.7188	18.26
	0.7283	18.50
47/64	0.7344	18.65
	0.7480	19.00
3/4	0.7500	19.05
49/64	0.7656	19.45
	0.7677	19.50
25/32	0.7812	19.84
	0.7874	20.00
51/64	0.7969	20.24
	0.8000	20.32
13/16	0.8125	20.64
	0.8268	21.00
53/64	0.8281	21.03
27/32	0.8438	21.43
	0.8464	21.50
	0.8500	21.59

Fraction of inch	Decimal inches	Milli-meters
55/64	0.8594	21.83
	0.8662	22.00
7/8	0.8750	22.23
	0.8859	22.50
57/64	0.8906	22.62
	0.9000	22.86
	0.9055	23.00
29/32	0.9062	23.02
59/64	0.9219	23.42
	0.9252	23.50
15/16	0.9375	23.81
	0.9449	24.00
	0.9500	24.13
61/64	0.9531	24 21
31/32	0.9688	24.61
63/64	0.9843	25.00
1	1.0000	25.40
	1.0236	26.00
	1.05	26.70
1-1/16	1.0625	26.99
	1.0630	27.00
	1.1000	27.94
	1.1024	28.00
1-1/8	1.1250	28.58
	1.1417	29.00
	1.1500	29.21
	1.1811	30.00
1-3/16	1.1875	30.16
	1.2000	30.48
	1.2205	31.00
1-1/4	1.2500	31.75
	1.2598	32.00
	1.2992	33.00
	1.3000	33.02
1-5/16	1.3125	33.34
	1.3386	34.00
	1.3500	39.29
1-3/8	1.3750	34.92
	1.3780	35.00
	1.4000	35.56
	1.4173	36.00
1-7/16	1.4375	36.51
	1.4500	36.83
	1.4567	37.00
	1.4961	38.00

Fraction of inch	Decimal inches	Milli-meters
1-1/2	1.5000	38.10
	1.5354	39.00
	1.5500	39.37
1-9/16	1.5625	39.69
	1.5748	40.00
	1.6000	40.64
	1.6142	41.00
1-5/8	1.6250	41.28
	1.6500	41.91
	1.6536	42.00
1-11/16	1.6875	42.86
	1.6929	43.00
	1.7000	43.18
	1.7323	44.00
1-3/4	1.7500	44.45
	1.7717	45.00
	1.8000	45.72
	1.8110	46.00
1-13/16	1.8125	46.04
	1.8500	46.99
	1.8504	47.00
1-7/8	1.8750	47.62
	1.8898	48.00
	1.9000	48.26
	1.9291	49.00
1-15/16	1.9375	49.21
	1.9500	49.53
	1.9685	50.00
2	2.0000	50.80
	2.0079	51.00
	2.0473	52.00
2-1/16	2.0625	52.39
	2.0866	53.00
	2.1000	53.34
2-1/8	2.1250	53.98
	2.1260	54.00
	2.1654	55.00
2-3/16	2.1875	55.56
	2.2000	55.88
	2.2047	56.00
	2.2441	57.00
2-1/4	2.2500	57.15
	2.2835	58.00
	2.3000	58.42

Fraction of inch	Decimal inches	Milli-meters
2-5/16	2.3125	58.74
	2.3228	59.00
	2.3622	60.00
2-3/8	2.3750	60.32
	2.4000	60.96
	2.4016	61.00
2-7/16	2.4375	61.92
	2.4410	62.00
	2.4803	63.00
2-1/2	2.5000	63.50
	2.5197	64.00
	2.5591	65.00
2-9/16	2.5625	65.09
	2.5984	66.00
	2.6000	66.04
2-5/8	2.6250	66.68
	2.6378	67.00
	2.6772	68.00
2-11/16	2.6875	68.26
	2.7000	68.58
	2.7166	69.00
2-3/4	2.7500	69.85
	2.7559	70.00
	2.7953	71.00
	2.8000	71.12
2-13/16	2.8125	71.44
	2.8347	72.00
	2.8740	73.00
2-7/8	2.8750	73.03
	2.9000	73.66
	2.9134	74.00
2-15/16	2.9375	74.61
	2.9528	75.00
	2.9922	76.00
3	3.0000	76.20

Numbers for large quantities

For amounts of anything above a million, the United States has a numbering system almost unique among nations. The U.S. system was copied from the French system, but the French later adopted the system used in England and Germany. The U.S. system multiplies the previous figure by 1,000. Example: a *billion* is 1,000 *millions*. But the European system multiplies by one million. Example: a British *billion* is a million *millions*.

	U.S. System		British System	
Name	**Description**	**No. of zeros**	**Description**	**No. of zeros**
million	1,000 thousands	6	1,000 thousands	6
milliard	none exists	—	1,000 millions	9
billion	1,000 millions	9	1,000,000 millions	12
trillion	1,000 billions	12	1,000,000 billions	18
quadrillion	1,000 trillions	15	1,000,000 trillions	24
quintillion	1,000 quadrillions	18	1,000,000 quadrillions	30
sextillion	1,000 quintillions	21	1,000,000 quintillions	36
septillion	1,000 sextillions	24	1,000,000 sextillions	42
octillion	1,000 septillions	27	1,000,000 septillions	48
nonillion	1,000 octillions	30	1,000,000 octillions	54
decillion	1,000 nonillions	33	1,000,000 nonillions	60
undecillion	1,000 decillions	36	1,000,000 decillions	66
duodecillion	1,000 undecillions	39	1,000,000 undecillions	72
tredecillion	1,000 duodecillions	42	1,000,000 duodecillions	78
quattuordecillion	1,000 tredecillions	45	1,000,000 tredecillions	84
quindecillion	1,000 quattordecillions	48	1,000,000 quattuordecillions	90
sexdecillion	1,000 quindecillions	51	1,000,000 quindecillions	96
septendecillion	1,000 sexdecillions	54	1,000,000 sexdecillions	102
octodecillion	1,000 septendecillions	57	1,000,000 septendecillions	108
novemdecillion	1,000 octodecillions	60	1,000,000 octodecillions	114
vignitillion	1,000 novemdecillions	63	1,000,000 novemdecillions	120

Numbers for scientific measurement

Scientists and engineers use prefixes before measurements to accurately and quickly express their magnitudes. Example: instead of saying "1,000 volts," one can say "kilovolt;" and instead of "one million watts," one can say "megawatt."

Prefix	Abbreviation	Multiplier
tera	T	10^{12} or 1,000,000,000,000
giga	G	10^{9} or 1,000,000,000
mega	M	10^{6} or 1,000,000
kilo	k	10^{3} or 1,000
hecto	h	10^{2} or 100
deka	da	10 or 10
deci	d	10^{-1} or .1
centi	c	10^{-2} or .01
milli	m	10^{-3} or .001
micro	μ	10^{-6} or .000001
nano	n	10^{-9} or .000000001
pico	p	10^{-12} or .000000000001
femto	f	10^{-15} or .000000000000001
atto	a	10^{-18} or .000000000000000001

Oven temperature equivalents

Degrees F.	Description
250 – 275	Very slow oven
300 – 325	Slow oven
350 – 375	Moderate oven
400 – 425	Hot oven
450 – 475	Very hot oven
500 – 525	Extremely hot oven

Source: The Quaker Oats Company.

Paint estimator

Find the width of your room along the top of this chart, and its length along the left side. Where the two columns intersect you will find the number of square feet of wall space in your room, assuming your ceilings are 8 feet high. (For ceiling heights of other than 8 feet, use the adjustment given at the bottom of the chart.) Deduct 20 square feet for every door and (unless you actually measure them) 10 square feet for every window. The resulting figure will help you buy the right amount of paint. (For ceilings, simply multiply width by length to obtain square feet.)

	Feet																	
Feet	**3**	**4**	**5**	**6**	**7**	**8**	**9**	**10**	**11**	**12**	**13**	**14**	**15**	**16**	**17**	**18**	**19**	**20**
3	96	112	128	144	160	176	192	208	224	240	256	272	288	304	320	336	352	368
4	112	128	144	160	176	192	208	224	240	256	272	288	304	320	336	352	368	384
5	128	144	160	176	192	208	224	240	256	272	288	304	320	336	352	368	384	400
6	144	160	176	192	208	224	240	256	272	288	304	320	336	352	368	384	400	416
7	160	176	192	208	224	240	256	272	288	304	320	336	352	368	384	400	416	432
8	176	192	208	224	240	256	272	288	304	320	336	352	368	384	400	416	432	448
9	192	208	224	240	256	272	288	304	320	336	352	368	384	400	416	432	448	464
10	208	224	240	256	272	288	304	320	336	352	368	384	400	416	432	448	464	480
11	224	240	256	272	288	304	320	336	352	368	384	400	416	432	448	464	480	496
12	240	256	272	288	304	320	336	352	368	384	400	416	432	448	464	480	496	512
13	256	272	288	304	320	336	352	368	384	400	416	432	448	464	480	496	512	528
14	272	288	304	320	336	352	368	384	400	416	432	448	464	480	496	512	528	544
15	288	304	320	336	352	368	384	400	416	432	448	464	480	496	512	528	544	560
16	304	320	336	352	368	384	400	416	432	448	464	480	496	512	528	544	560	576
17	320	336	352	368	384	400	416	432	448	464	480	496	512	528	544	560	576	592

18	336	352	368	384	400	416	432	448	464	480	496	512	528	544	560	576	592	608
19	352	368	384	400	416	432	448	464	480	496	512	528	544	560	576	592	608	624
20	368	384	400	416	432	448	464	480	496	512	528	544	560	576	592	608	624	640
21	384	400	416	432	448	464	480	496	512	528	544	560	576	592	608	624	640	656
22	400	416	432	448	464	480	496	512	528	544	560	576	592	608	624	640	656	672
23	416	432	448	464	480	496	512	528	544	560	576	592	608	624	640	656	672	688
24	432	448	464	480	496	512	528	544	560	576	592	608	624	640	656	672	688	704
25	448	464	480	496	512	528	544	560	576	592	608	624	640	656	672	688	704	720

For ceilings that are not 8 feet high, multiply the above results by this factor *before* deducting for doors and windows:

7½ feet: 0.9
9 feet: 1.1
9½ feet: 1.2
10 feet: 1.25
10½ feet: 1.3
11 feet: 1.4
11½ feet: 1.44
12 feet: 1.5

Paint selector

There is a beautiful, durable, easy-to-apply paint product for every paintable surface—and in any color your heart desires. This table will help you select the best finishing material for your interior surfaces.

A = excellent choice
B = OK under proper conditions, but not the overall preferred paint
X = not generally recommended

Surfaces	Flat paint	Satin enamel	Semi-gloss	Porch & floor enamel	Quick-Dry Enamel	Varnish (especially urethane)	Wood stains
WALL							
Plaster	A	A	B	X	X	X	X
Wallboard	A	A	B	X	X	X	X
Masonry	B	A	A	B	X	X	X
CEILINGS							
Plaster	A	B	B	X	X	X	X
Masonry	A	B	B	X	X	X	X
Acoustical	A	A	B	X	B	X	X
TRIM							
Wood	B	B	A	X	A	A	A
Metal plastic	B	B	A	X	A	B	A
FLOORS							
Wood (painted)	X	X	X	A	X	X	X
Concrete	X	X	X	A	X	B	X
Hardwood	X	X	X	X	X	A	B
MISCELLANEOUS							
Wood paneling	X	X	X	X	X	A	B
Furniture	X	B	B	X	A	A	A

Pipe sizes

Trade names for pipes have very little to do with their real size. Example: a pipe that has a ½-inch inside diameter is *not* known as a ½-inch pipe; it is a ⅜-inch pipe. This chart will help you figure out the trade name for your pipes no matter which dimension you are able to measure. (All figures are in inches.)

Trade name	Inside diameter	Outside diameter	Circumference
Iron Pipe			
¼-inch	3/8	9/16	1-11/16
⅜-inch	1/2	11/16	2-1/8
½-inch	5/8	13/16	2-5/8
¾-inch	13/16	1-1/16	3-5/16
1-inch	1-1/16	1-5/16	4-1/8
1¼-inch	1-3/8	1-11/16	5-3/16
1½-inch	1-5/8	1-7/8	6
2-inch	2-1/16	2-3/8	7-7/16
Copper Pipe			
⅜-inch	7/16	1/2	1-9/16
½-inch	9/16	5/8	1-15/16
¾-inch	13/16	7/8	2-3/4
1-inch	1	1-1/8	3-9/16
1¼-inch	1-1/4	1-3/8	4-5/16
1½-inch	1-1/2	1-5/8	5-1/8

Plants that are poisonous

Name	Description	Poisonous parts	Antidote
Baneberry (snakeberry)	Perennial herb, 1–2 feet high, large leaves, small white flowers in spring. Red or white berries clustered on terminal stalks, each on short fleshy stem.	Root stock, sap, berries: produce nausea, violent vomiting. Can affect heart, increase pulse rate, cause dizziness. Fatalities reported.	Call doctor. Have patient vomit.
American bittersweet (European bittersweet, blue or black nightshade, woody nightshade, poison berry)	Woody climbing or reclining herb, slender stems, dark green pointed leaves (may be purplish when young). Clusters of white or purple-white flowers on 5-pointed wheel-shaped base. Bright red to scarlet berries on European bittersweet, purple or black berries on American bittersweet.	Chiefly leaves, unripe fruits. Berries, if several are eaten. Cause throat burning, nausea, dizziness, eye dilation, convulsions, muscle weakness.	Call doctor. Have patient vomit.
Bloodroot	Low-growing perennial herb, appears in early spring in moist wooded areas. Stalk has single large-lobed leaf, many-petaled white flower.	Underground stems, roots, and their red juice. Cause intense burning of mouth, throat, and stomach; vomiting. If absorbed, can cause coma and temporary paralysis.	Call doctor. Have patient vomit, then give warm milk.
Castor bean (castor-oil plant, palma christi)	Grow to 8 feet. Large showy palmlike dark green leaves on long stalks. Soft spiny fruits, shiny seeds shaped like tick insect, with attractive white to brown or black striations.	Beans or seeds. Cause nausea, vomiting, intestinal cramps, stupor, sometimes convulsions and circulatory collapse several hours later.	Call doctor. Have patient vomit.
Christmas rose (black hellebore)	Perennial evergreen herb, black underground stem and roots. Each year (winter in warm climates) has one leaf and flower stalk form with one or two large purplish-white flowers. Flower has yellow center, 5 petals.	Leaves, roots, and juice inflame skin; cause tingling and numbing in mouth, violent vomiting.	Call doctor. Wash juice off skin at once with warm soapy water. If eaten, have patient vomit.

(spurge olive)	in clusters along branches in spring before leaves develop. Summer bright red berries, each with one seed. (Some have white to yellow flowers, yellow to orange berries.)	cause fatalities among children.) Causes burning in mouth, cramps in stomach, intestines. If absorbed, can produce kidney inflammation.	vomit.
Deadly nightshade (black cherry)	Perennial bushy herb, 3–4 feet high. Branching stems with dark green pointed leaves. Lavender to purple bell-shaped flowers. Black cherrylike fruits.	Roots, leaves, stems. Causes drying of mouth, dilation of eye pupils, rapid heartbeat, central nervous system depression. Very poisonous.	Call doctor. Have patient vomit at once if eaten. Wash exposed skin with soapy water.
Foxglove (digitalis)	Biennial flowers on long erect stems with many small bell-shaped flowerettes, white-lavender or purple. (Often cultivated in gardens.)	Leaves and seeds. Causes vomiting, nausea, dizziness up to several hours after ingestion. Can cause heart failure.	Call doctor. Have patient vomit.
Green hellebore (false hellebore, Indian poke)	Found in swamps, moist meadows, along streams. Begins like skunk cabbage but grows 6–8 feet high on stout stalks. Broad-leaved with parallel vein markings. Small greenish-white flowers on a branching top.	Roots, leaves, and seeds. Causes salivation, abdominal pain, attempts to vomit. Large quantities cause cold, clammy skin, depressed circulation, possible death.	Call doctor. Have patient vomit if he appears calm and is conscious. If in shock, use standard first aid.
Jimson weed (thornapple, Jamestown weed) (angel's trumpet, a similar plant, is less poisonous)	Annual herb, 3–4 feet high. Stems (green or purple) branch, trumpet-shaped white flowers or thorny fruits form in forks of branches. Seeds are brown-black, kidney-shaped.	Roots, leaves, seeds. Causes drying of mouth, dilation of eye pupils, rapid heartbeat, nervous system depression. (Handling leaves can poison.)	Call doctor. Have patient vomit; wash hands with soapy water.

Larkspur (delphinium, lark's claw, knight's spur)	Garden annual or perennial; flowers usually white or purple on erect stalks. Plant 2–4 feet high.	Leaves, seeds. Causes mouth tingling followed by excitation, severe depression. (Poisoned animals seem to have symptoms of tetany.)	Call doctor. Have patient vomit.
Lily of the valley	Perennial low-growing herb. Broad leaves have parallel vein markings. Small white nodding bell-shaped flowers, fragrant, form on one side of slender stalk. Fruits are red to orange fleshy berries.	Roots, leaves, fruits. Stimulates heart muscles, causes dizziness and vomiting in 1 to 2 hours if large quantities are eaten.	Call doctor. Have patient vomit.
Monkshood (aconite, friar's cap, wolfsbane)	Perennial herb to 3–4 feet high. Several violet-blue flowers, shaped like monk's hood, on each stalk. Tiny seeds.	Roots, seeds; leaves may be harmful if eaten. Cause heart slowing, tingling and numbness of lips and tongue, irregular pulse, dim vision, heart failure.	Call doctor. Keep patient warm, lying horizontally with head and feet level.
Mushroom (many varieties are poisonous, so don't eat any that grow wild unless an expert has okayed them)	Found in woody places, along roadsides, at bases of trees, in waste places.	If a mushroom is poisonous, all its parts are poisonous. May cause sweating, wheezing, irregular breath and heartbeat. Some varieties can be fatal within hours.	Call doctor. Have patient vomit.
Poison hemlock (poison parsley)	Biennial weed. Leaves parsleylike, dark green. Grows to 5 feet or more. Roots resemble parsnip; crushed leaves and roots smell like parsnip. Very small white flowers on umbrellalike stalks. In gardens, fields, and along roads. (Don't mistake for parsley, parsnip, or anise.)	Leaves and fruits during flowering, as well as older roots. Causes burning in mouth and throat, then muscle weakness, stupor, paralysis of arms and chest, possible respiratory failure, death	Call doctor. Have patient vomit.

Poison ivy (poison oak)	Woody climbing vine or low-branching shrub, both found in woods, along fences, walks. Leaves turn showy red and yellow in fall. Poison oak's leaf looks oaklike; poison ivy's is shiny with 3 to a cluster. Flowers yellowish-green to white.	All parts (even tiny plant hairs and smoke if leaves are burned). Causes severe skin blistering, inflammation.	Wash lavishly with soapy water using alkali laundry soap; lather abundantly. (Don't use soaps that contain oil or greases.) See druggist for further remedy. If severe dermatitis, call doctor.
Pokeweed (pigeonberry, American nightshade, ink berries, scoke, red ink plant)	Perennial weed, grows to 4 feet. Large fleshy root system, thick stems, light green leaves. Greenish-white flowers on spikes. Green berry clusters turn red, purple, then black; red juice.	All parts, particularly roots, shoots, unripe berries. Slow poisoning (1 to 2 hours later) becomes violent for a long time: nausea, vomiting, drowsiness, impaired vision. Large amounts can cause coma, death.	Call doctor. Have patient vomit.
Water hemlock (cowbane, beaver poison)	Perennial herb, grows to 5 feet or more. In swampy, moist areas. Roots resemble parsnip; rootlets resemble small sweet potatoes and yield yellowish aromatic oil when cut open. White flowers on small umbrellalike stalks.	Mostly the roots, but also above-ground parts. Causes severe stomach pain, frenzy, vomiting, frothing at the mouth (at times bloody), irregular breathing, convulsions, death.	Call doctor. Have patient vomit.
Yew (groundhemlock)	Evergreen tree or shrub often used in garden or as hedge. Bright red fleshy berries, sometimes with a large hole in the end giving appearance of cup. (Berries attract children.)	All parts. (Red berries are least harmful.) Causes nausea, vomiting, diarrhea, abdominal pain, circulatory failure, breathing difficulty.	Call doctor. Have patient vomit.

Source: U.S. Department of Health and Human Services, Bureau of Product Safety.

Plywood grades

Plywood is a flat panel built up of sheets of veneer called plies, united under pressure by adhesives to create a panel with a bond between plies as strong as, or stronger than, ordinary wood. Plywood is constructed of an odd number of layers, with grain of adjacent layers perpendicular to each other. Interior as well as exterior plywood is graded by manufacturers. The grade of the two outside veneers is stamped onto each sheet.

A: Smooth and paintable; may be clear-coated for rugged natural finish. Neatly made repairs permissible.

B: Solid surface veneer. Circular repair plugs and tight knots permitted.

C: Knotholes to 1 inch. Occasional knotholes ½ inch larger permitted, provided total width of all knots and knotholes within a specified section does not exceed certain limits. Limited splits permitted.

C/plgd: Improved C veneer (C Plugged) with splits limited to ⅛ inch in width and knotholes and borer holes limited to ¼ inch by ½ inch.

D: Permits knots and knotholes to 2½-inch width and ½ inch larger under certain specified limits. Limited splits permitted.

Grade	Face	Back	Inner plies	Applications
For exterior uses				
A-A	A	A	C	Outdoors, where appearance of both faces is important.
A-B	A	B	C	Substitute for A-A when appearance of one side is less important.
A-C	A	C	C	Soffits, fences, base for coatings.
B-C	B	C	C	For utility uses such as farm buildings, some kinds of fences, base for coatings, etc.
C-C/plgd	C/plgd	C	C	Excellent base for tile and vinyl, backing for wall coverings, high-performance coatings.
C-C	C	C	C	Unsanded, for backing and rough construction exposed to weather.
B-B Plyform	B	B	C	Concrete forms. Reuse until wood wears out.
For interior uses				
A-A	A	A	D	Cabinet doors, built-ins, furniture where both sides will show.
A-B	A	B	D	Substitute for A-A. Face is finished grade but back is solid and smooth.

Grade	Face	Back	Inner plies	Applications
A-D	A	D	D	Finish grade face for paneling, built-ins, backing.
B-D	B	D	D	Utility grade for backing, cabinet sides, etc.
C-D	C	D	D	Sheathing and structural use such as temporary enclosures, subfloor, etc. Unsanded.
Underlayment	C/plgd	D	C and D	For underlayment or combination subfloor-underlayment under tile, carpet, etc.

Source: American Plywood Association.

Roman numerals

Used mostly for decorative purposes and for copyright notices in movies these days, Roman numbering is straightforward if cumbersome. You simply add the values of each integer—unless a smaller integer precedes a larger one, in which case you subtract. Example: XCIX is ten subtracted from 100 and then 1 subtracted from 10; therefore it equals 99.

Number	Roman numeral	Number	Roman numeral	Number	Roman numeral
1	I	32	XXXII	500	D
2	II	40	XL	700	DCC
3	III	43	XLIII	716	DCCXVI
4	IV	50	L	900	CM
5	V	54	LIV	1,000	M
6	VI	60	LX	1,001	MI
7	VII	65	LXV	1,900	MCM
8	VIII	70	LXX	1,980	MCMLXXX
9	IX	76	LXXVI	1,987	MCMLXXXVII
10	X	80	LXXX	1,990	XMM
11	XI	87	LXXXVII	1,999	IMM
12	XII	90	XC	2,000	MM
13	XIII	98	XCVIII	5,000	$\overline{V}$
14	XIV	100	C	10,000	$\overline{X}$
15	XV	109	CIX	50,000	$\overline{L}$
16	XVI	110	CX	100,000	$\overline{C}$
20	XX	150	CL	125,000	$\overline{CXXV}$
21	XXI	200	CC	500,000	$\overline{D}$
30	XXX	400	CD	1,000,000	$\overline{M}$

Safety checklist for the home

Entrances

Lighting: Outside and inside porch light switch advised.
Handrails: Needed if 2 or more outside steps.
Steps: Should be finished with nonslip materials.
Locks: Should be adequate and in good repair.

Passages

Door glass: Should be safety glass.
Doormat: Should be placed so it won't be tripped over.
Floors: Should be even, never polished under mats.
Runners: Should have nonslip backing.
Passageway: Should be free of obstructions.
Lighting: Good lighting advised.

Living room

Floors: Keep carpets and rugs unwrinkled; use nonslip polish.
Lighting: Keep bulbs and shades clean.
Outlets: Have enough for all recreational use without needing extension cords. Avoid running cords where they may be tripped on.
Fireplaces: Should have full-size screen or glass guard.
Chimney: Should be cleaned regularly.
Windows: Keep window catches and sash cords in good repair; see that curtains are not near fire source.
Furniture: Should have rounded corners and firm legs.

Kitchen

Ranges: Switches should be where they can't be bumped; pot handles should always be prevented from protruding over edge.
Electricity: Plugs, switches, and wiring should be kept in good condition; ground fault interrupters are preferred.
Appliances: Should be out of reach of young children.
Cleaning supplies: Should be out of reach of young children.
Kitchen tools: Keep sharp tools out of reach of young children.
Personal safety: Pot holders should be at hand; cooking utensils should have heat-resistant handles; grease and water spills should be mopped at once; stepstools should be used to reach high places.

Dining room

Layout: Keep doorways clear.

Floors: Keep floor coverings in good repair.

Electricity: Plugs, switches, and wiring should be kept in good condition. Have enough outlets for all appliances.

Appliances: Plugs and sockets should be in good repair.

Furniture: Children's high chair should have good safety catches.

Table coverings: Should not hang so low as to cause possible pulling or tripping.

Stairs and landing

Stair covering: Should be tacked firmly in place.

Banisters: Should be firm and strong.

Lighting: Good lighting advised; two-way top and bottom switch suggested.

Passageways: Should be kept free of obstructions.

Bedrooms

Floors: Keep floor coverings in good repair.

Windows: Keep window catches in good repair. For children's rooms use safety catches to keep window from opening too far.

Beds: Electric blankets should be kept unwrinkled and unfolded while in use.

Lighting: Switches should enable user to light the way into the room and to light the room from the bed(s).

Heating: Electric heaters should be in good repair and kept away from curtains and bed coverings.

General safety: Never smoke in bed.

Bathroom

Bath: Should have handle; nonslip floor preferred.

Appliances: Should not be turned on when bathing (radios, hair dryers, etc.).

Drugs: Cabinet should have lock if young children in house; razor blades should be disposed of carefully.

Locks: Can hold up help if accident occurs; not advised, especially if young children in house.

General safety: Never touch electric switches when wet; check bath water temperature for children.

Sewing needle and thread sizes

Fabrics	Hand needle size	Machine Needle size	Machine Stitches per inch	Thread sizes
SHEER Net, chiffon, voile, batiste, crepe, ninon, dotted Swiss, organdy, fine linen, marquisette.	9, 10	Finest	16	70 black. 70,100,120,150 white
MEDIUM Satin, taffeta, wool, corduroy, gingham, chintz, jersey, pique, flannel, shantung.	7,8,9	Medium	12	50,60,70
MEDIUM-HEAVY Drapery and quilted fabrics, terry, denim, felt, velvet, tweed, suiting, coating.	6	Medium-coarse	10	36, 40
HEAVY Unpholstery, heavy denim, ticking, sailcloth.	4,5	Coarse	8	24, 30, 36
VERY HEAVY Sewing on coat and suit buttons; duck, canvas, awning cloth, rug bindings.	1,2,3	Coarsest	6	8, 10, 20, or (by hand) button & carpet thread

Source: Coats & Clark, Inc.

Shoe wear delineator

Your old shoes can guide your selection of new ones. Study your worn shoes and compare the wear to this chart.

Wear	Possible cause
Outer sole curls a lot at toe. (It should curl a bit off the ground.)	Shoe is too long.
Sole worn unevenly.	Shoe is too short, especially the distance from heel to ball.
Upper bulge over sole line.	Shoe is too narrow.
Heel pushes under or new lifts required often.	Shoe is too short.
Heel wears on inside.	Foot weakness. (Slight wear at back or outside line is normal.)
Shoe wears at tip of toe.	Shoe is too short.
Inside lining of heel is worn.	Shoe may be too long.
Shoe worn out of shape.	Wrong size; improper walk; foot weakness.
Inside sole is worn.	Shoe is too tight.
Pockets formed for toes.	Shoe is too tight.
Shoe puckered or wrinkled behind the ball along arch.	Overall length of shoe may be proper, but proportion is not. Shoe is not long enough from ball to heel.

Source: North Dakota State University Extension Service.

Siding estimator

This chart shows how to estimate how much exterior siding to purchase for your home. For openings such as doors and windows subtract only half of the actual openings you measure, as the chart shows, to allow for actual waste.

House area

Length of:

Front wall ____________

Side wall(l) +____________

Side wall(r) +____________

Rear wall +____________

Other wall +____________

Other wall +____________

Total length: =____________

Height of walls: ×____________ (multiply)

SUBTOTAL A: =____________

Gable #1:

Length ____________

Height ×____________ (multiply)

=____________ Divide by 2 =____________

Gable #2:

Length ____________

Height ×____________ (multiply)

=____________ Divide by 2 =____________

SUBTOTAL B (Gable #1 + #2): ____________

Total of window and
door areas (height × width):____________Divide by 2 =____________
SUBTOTAL C

Siding required:

Subtotal A ____________

Subtotal B +____________ (add)

=____________

Subtotal C −____________ (subtract)

Siding required: ____________•Square feet

Spices: which for what

Name	Source	Description	Uses
Allspice	Guatemala Jamaica Mexico	Brown whole berries or aromatic powder with flavor like mixture of cloves and cinnamon.	Baked goods Fruit dishes Pickles, relishes, marinades Yellow vegetables
Aniseed	Mediterranean countries	Herb seed with flavor and aroma like licorice.	Soups Cheeses and canapes Stews Candies Hot beverages
Basil	Bulgaria France Hungary USA	Bits of dried leaves with pungent, mildly aromatic, very deep flavor.	Italian-style pasta sauces Cooked vegetables such as tomato and squash Seafood, poultry Salads
Bay leaf	Turkey	Large, deep green leaves with sharply pungent aroma and peppery taste with mint aftertaste.	Soups Stews Marinades Occasionally in casseroles of meat, fish, poultry
Caraway seed	Holland Denmark Poland	Tiny brown seeds with tangy, almost nutty flavor.	Rye bread Sauerkraut Cheese dips Casseroles

Name	Source	Description	Uses
Cardamom seed	India Guatemala	Tan or green-colored pods full of tiny brown seeds with strong, sweetly pungent taste and pleasant aroma.	Baked goods such as coffee cake, cookies, buns, pumpkin pie, apple pie Ground into coffee
Chervil	USA France	Similar in appearance and flavor to parsley, but with faint hint of licorice.	Salads Sauces Stuffing Omelets
Cinnamon	Indonesia China	Whole brown sticks or light brown powder with soft aroma and distinctive sharp taste.	Baked goods such as apple pie, pumpkin pie Puddings Sauces
Cloves	Zanzibar Indonesia Madagascar	Pointed bud and stem, or reddish powder, with peppery, minty aroma and taste.	Whole, pressed into ham or pork Whole, pickling and marinades Fruit desserts, stews, gravies, vegetables such as yams Baked goods Beverages
Cumin seed	Mediterranean area	Usually a yellow-tan powder (ground from seeds) with light, pungent aroma but distinctive peppery taste.	Spanish cooking Mexican cooking Indian cooking Spicy Chinese cooking Corn bread Chili
Curry powder	USA	Blend of sundry spices: usually ground chili pepper, cumin, oregano, garlic, salt; often cloves, allspice, onion. The resulting tan powder is hot, pungent, powerful.	Curry sauce for eggs, fish, meat, and occasionally vegetables Clam and fish chowders Split pea soup Stewed tomatoes

	India	attached, having mild carawaylike taste but little aroma.	Stuffing Vegetables such as cabbage, beans, cauliflower, potatoes Salad dressings or salads Fish Delicate sauces
Garlic	USA	Tiny white corm with mildly pungent aroma and gentle but distinctive flavor, or powder ground from dried garlic with harsher flavor.	Meats and fish Casseroles Soups, sauces Salads and dressings Bread
Ginger	Jamaica India Nigeria China	Whole, tan root or light brown powder with sharp and pungent, but pleasant flavor and aroma.	Baked goods such as cakes, cookies Beef or chicken dishes Sauces Chinese cooking
Mace	West Indies Indonesia	Ground yellow powder from one layer of nutmeg fruit, with nutmeglike flavor but heavier.	Fruit cakes Pound cakes Cherry pie Sweet vegetables Sauces and chowders Creamed spinach Chicken
Marjoram	France Egypt	Greyish-green bits of leaves with biting aroma but mild peppery taste in cooked foods, obvious biting taste in salads.	Salads Herbed breads Green vegetables Roasted meat, fish, poultry

Name	Source	Description	Uses
Mustard seed	USA Canada England Denmark	Tiny yellow-brown seeds or ground powder with little aroma but sharp taste when moist.	Seed: pickles, salads Cheese dishes Ham salad Deviled eggs
Nutmeg	West Indies Indonesia	Whole brown round berries or ground brown powder with sweet, nutty aroma and taste.	Baked goods such as pies, cakes, cookies Puddings, custards Eggnog Creamed corn, creamed spinach Seafood Chicken
Oregano	Mexico Greece Turkey	Bits of dull green leaves with strong aroma and taste of "pizza."	Pizza Italian cooking and sauces Cheese dishes Salads Meat and fish
Paprika	USA Spain Hungary	Richly colored red powder with slightly sweet but biting taste.	Deviled eggs Cheese dishes such as Welsh rarebit Sour cream dips Bisques Garnish on cottage cheese
Pepper, Black	Brazil India Indonesia	Wrinkled whole peppercorns or ground powder with heavy, pungent, unique aroma and flavor.	Salads Meats Vegetables Some cakes, cookies

Pepper, White	India Indonesia Malaysia	Lighter-colored and lighter-flavored than black pepper.	As above, but for lighter-flavored or lighter-colored dishes
Pepper, Red	USA Mexico China	Crushed whole peppers or ground cayenne pepper, red in color and very heavily flavored.	Pizza Italian-style sauces Mexican cooking Dips, sauces, soups Meats, fish Marinades
Poppy seed	Holland Romania Turkey	Tiny blue-grey seeds with pleasant nutty taste but very little aroma.	Topping in baked goods Major ingredient in poppy seed cake Noodles Cheesecake Cole slaw
Rosemary	France Portugal Yugoslavia	Narrow, pointed green leaves with sharp, obvious aroma and bittersweet taste.	Lamb, chicken, beef, pork Sauces for fish Salads Eggplant, beans, squash, mushrooms
Saffron	Spain	Expensive yellow strands of flower stigma that bring rich yellow color and pleasantly bitter taste. Fortunately, a bit goes a long way.	Rice Chicken Seafoods Indian cooking
Sage	Albania Yugoslavia Turkey	Fluffy, light yellow-green powder from ground or rubbed leaves, with pleasant aroma and distinctive strong taste.	Green beans Chicken, meats Stuffing Salad Soups Omelets

Name	Source	Description	Uses
Savory	France Yugoslavia	Brown-green dried leaves with sharp, minty aroma and taste.	Beans Salads Soups Sauces Eggs Meats
Sesame seed	Central America Ethiopia	Small ivory-white seeds with bland texture and taste until toasted or baked; then the taste is pleasantly nutty.	Topping for baked goods such as buns, breads, cakes, cookies, cream pies Stuffing Vegetable butters Fried chicken Middle Eastern cooking
Tarragon	USA France Yugoslavia	Bits of light green leaves with sweetly pungent aroma and taste, offering just a hint of licorice.	Salads and dressings Casseroles, especially for chicken Tartar sauce
Thyme	France Spain	Bits of grey-green leaves with distinctive aromatic pungency.	Chowders, especially seafood Stuffings Cream sauces Onions, eggplants, celery
Turmeric	Haiti Peru India	Ground orange-yellow root with saffronlike color and taste—slightly bitter.	Rice Chicken Seafoods Eggs Pickles and relishes

Spot and stain removal from carpets

Successful spot cleaning depends on quick and correct treatment. Locate the stain and its recommended cleaning method number on the index below. Cleaning method directions follow.

Spot or stain	Cleaning method
Alcohol, Beer, Mixed Drinks	1
Blood	1
Butter, Margarine	1
Candy, other than chocolate	1
Catsup, Tomato Juice	1
Chocolate, Cocoa	1
Cigarette Burns	4
Coffee, black	1
Coffee, with cream	1
Coffee, with sugar	1
Correction Fluid	2, 5
Cosmetics	2
Egg	1
Fruit, Berry Stains	1
Grease	2
Glue, household	1
Glue, model	4
Gravy	1, 2
Gum	4
Ink, ballpoint	2
Ink, non-water soluble	2, 5
Ink, water soluble	1
Iodine	5
Lipstick	2
Mercurochrome, Merthiolate	3
Mildew	1, 5
Milk, Cream, Ice Cream	1
Mud	4
Mustard	1, 2
Nail Polish	4
Oil, clear vegetable	1
Oil, machine, mineral	2
Paint, water base, wet	1
Paint, oil base, wet	4
Paint, dry	5
Peanut Butter	1
Perfume	3
Rust	1, 5
Sauces, Salad Dressing	1
Shoe Polish	2
Soft Drinks	1

Spot or stain	Cleaning method
Sugar, Jelly, Jam, Syrup	1, 2
Tar, Asphalt	2
Tea	1
Toothpaste	1
Urine	4
Vomit	1
Water	4
Wax, candle	4
Wax, car, floor, furniture	2
Wine	1

Carpet spot cleaning methods

Locate your spot and cleaning method number on the chart, then follow the directions below. If your spot has two methods listed, use the first method, then the second method only if some stain remains. Pretest all cleaners on an inconspicuous part of the carpet.

METHOD #1 Foodstuffs, starches, and sugars

Remove excess material by blotting up liquids and scraping up solids. Sponge with cool water and blot. Apply carpet shampoo (foam type or concentrated liquid, diluted 1 part shampoo to 4 parts water) with a soft brush or turkish towel. Let the area dry, then vacuum. Repeat if necessary.

METHOD #2 Oily materials and grease

Remove excess stain by blotting up liquids and scraping up solids. Apply spot cleaner or dry cleaning solvent according to product directions. (If spot cleaner dries to a powder, vacuum before continuing.) Apply carpet shampoo (foam type or concentrated liquid, diluted 1 part shampoo to 4 parts water) with a brush or turkish towel. Let the area dry, then vacuum. Repeat if necessary.

METHOD #3 Alcohol base antiseptics and perfume

Remove excess material by blotting up liquids and scraping up solids. Sponge with a dilution of alcohol and water and blot *quickly*. Repeat until no stain color is absorbed into the blotting towel. Apply carpet shampoo (foam type or concentrated liquid, diluted 1 part shampoo to 4 parts water) with a brush or turkish towel. Let area dry, then vacuum.

METHOD #4 Special treatments

Cigarette burns—For light burns brush area lightly, then carefully clip away charred tufts. Shampoo, let dry, and vacuum. Severe burns need repair or replacement.

Glue, model—After removing excess, carefully apply nail polish remover by drops to soften glue. Scrape away. Shampoo, let dry, and vacuum.

Gum—Remove as much as possible by scraping. "Freeze" the residue with ice cubes in a plastic bag. Scrape off brittle gum. Shampoo, let dry, and vacuum.

Mud—Scrape up as much wet mud as possible and allow residue to dry completely. Vacuum well, then shampoo. Let area dry and vacuum again.

Nail Polish—Remove excess and apply nail polish remover by drops to soften, then scrape away. Shampoo, let dry, and vacuum.

Paint, oil base, wet—After removing excess paint, carefully apply turpentine or paint thinner and blot repeatedly. Shampoo, let dry, and vacuum.

Urine—Blot up excess. Sponge with cool water and blot. Sponge with white vinegar and blot well. Shampoo, let dry, and vacuum.

Water—Mop or blot as much as possible. Dry carpet quickly to prevent rot or mildew. Once dry, shampoo lightly, let dry, then vacuum.

Wax, candle—Remove excess by scraping. Cover with several layers of paper toweling and carefully press with a warm iron until all wax is removed. Shampoo, let dry, and vacuum.

METHOD #5

Contact a commercial carpet and rug cleaner for advice.

Source: Bissell Inc.

Spot and stain removal from upholstery

Successful spot cleaning depends on quick and correct treatment. Most fabrics *except* velvet, silk, and satin may be cleaned at home. Locate the stain and its recommended cleaning method number on the index below. Cleaning method directions follow.

Spot or stain	Cleaning method
Alcohol, Beer, Mixed Drinks	1
Blood	1
Butter, Margarine	1
Candy, Chocolate, Cocoa	1
Catsup, Tomato Juice	1
Cigarette Burns	5
Coffee, black	1
Coffee, with cream	1
Coffee, with sugar	1
Correction Fluid	2, 5
Cosmetics	2
Egg	1
Fruit, Berry Stains	1
Grease	2
Glue, household	1
Glue, model	5
Gravy	1, 5

Spot or stain	Cleaning method
Gum	4
Ink, ballpoint	5
Ink, non-water soluble	5
Ink, water soluble	1
Iodine	5
Lipstick	2
Mercurochrome, Merthiolate	3, 5
Mildew	1, 5
Milk, Cream, Ice Cream	1
Mud	4
Mustard	1, 2
Nail Polish	5
Oil, clear vegetable	1
Oil, machine, mineral	2
Paint, waterbase, wet	1
Paint, oil base, wet	5
Paint, dry	5
Peanut Butter	1
Perfume	3
Rust	1, 5
Sauces, Salad Dressing	1
Shoe Polish	2
Soft Drinks	1
Sugar, Jelly, Jam, Syrup	1, 2
Tar, Asphalt	2
Tea	1
Toothpaste	1
Urine	4
Vomit	1
Wax, candle	4
Wax, car, floor, furniture	2
Wine	1

Upholstery spot cleaning methods

Locate your spot and cleaning method number on the chart, then follow the directions below. If your spot has two methods listed, use the first method, then the second method only if some stain remains. Pretest all cleaners. Velvet, silk, and satin require commercial cleaning.

METHOD #1 Foodstuffs, starches, and sugars.

Remove excess material by blotting up liquids and scraping up solids. Sponge lightly with cool water and blot. Apply upholstery shampoo (foam type or concentrated liquid, diluted 1 part shampoo to 2 parts water) with a soft brush or turkish towel. Let the area dry thoroughly, then vacuum. Repeat if necessary.

METHOD #2 Oily materials and grease.

Remove excess material by blotting up liquids and scraping up solids. Carefully apply a spot cleaner or dry cleaning solvent according to product directions. (If spot cleaner dries to a powder, vacuum before continuing.) Apply upholstery shampoo (foam type or concentrated liquid, diluted 1 part shampoo to 2 parts water) with a soft brush or turkish towel. Let the area dry thoroughly, then vacuum. Repeat if necessary.

METHOD #3 Alcohol base antiseptics and perfume.

Remove excess material by blotting up liquids and scraping up solids. Sponge with a dilution of alcohol and water and blot *quickly*. Repeat until no stain color is absorbed into the blotting towel. Apply upholstery shampoo (foam type or concentrated liquid, diluted 1 part shampoo to 2 parts water) with a soft brush or turkish towel. Let area dry, then vacuum.

METHOD #4 Special treatments.

Gum—After removing as much as possible by scraping, "freeze" the residue with ice cubes in a plastic bag. Scrape off brittle gum. Remove any remaining gum by applying a spot cleaner or dry cleaning solvent. Shampoo, let dry, and vacuum.

Mud—Scrape up as much wet mud as possible and allow residue to dry completely. Vacuum well, then shampoo. Let area dry thoroughly and vacuum again.

Urine—Blot up excess, sponge with cool water and blot. Sponge with white vinegar and blot. Shampoo, let dry, and vacuum.

Wax, candle—Remove excess by scraping and "freeze" residue with ice cubes in a plastic bag. Scrape off brittle wax. Shampoo, let dry, and vacuum.

METHOD #5

Contact a commercial upholstery cleaner for advice.

Source: Bissell Inc.

Wallboard joint compound and tape estimator

In finishing newly applied wallboard (gypsum or plaster board), you will require about this much tape and joint compound.

Wallboard (square feet)	Ready-mixed joint compound (gallons)	Wallboard tape
100–200	1	2 60-ft. rolls
300–400	2	3 60-ft. rolls
500–600	3	1 250-ft. roll
700–800	4	1 250-ft. roll and 1 60-ft. roll
800–1,000	5	1 500-ft. roll

Source: *How to Improve Damn Near Everything Around Your Home,* Peterson and Kesselman-Turkel.

Wallpaper estimator

Measure the length of all four walls, add them together, and find that figure (or the next-largest one) in the left-hand column. Deduct 1 single roll for every 2 doorways and for every 60 square feet of window area.

Distance around room (feet)	Single rolls for wall areas	Height of ceiling		Number of yards for borders	Single rolls for ceilings
	8 feet	9 feet	10 feet		
28	8	8	10	11	2
30	8	8	10	11	2
32	8	8	10	12	2
34	8	10	10	13	4
36	8	10	10	13	4
38	10	10	12	14	4
40	10	10	12	15	4
42	10	12	12	15	4
44	10	12	14	16	4
46	12	12	14	17	6
48	12	12	14	17	6
50	12	14	14	18	6
52	12	14	16	19	6
54	14	14	16	19	6
56	14	14	16	20	8
58	14	16	18	21	8
60	14	16	18	21	8
62	14	16	20	22	8
64	16	18	20	23	8
66	16	18	20	23	10
68	16	18	20	24	10
70	16	20	20	25	10
72	18	20	20	25	12
74	18	20	22	26	12
76	18	20	22	27	12
78	18	20	22	27	14
80	20	20	24	28	14
82	20	22	24	29	14
84	20	22	24	30	16
86	20	22	24	30	16
88	20	22	26	31	16
90	20	24	26	32	18

Source: The Reardon Company.

Weights and measures equivalents

Length:			
1 foot	=	12	inches
1 yard	=	3	feet
	=	36	inches
1 (statute) mile	=	5,280	feet
	=	1,760	yards
100 centimeters	=	1	meter
1,000 meters	=	1	kilometer
Area:			
1 square foot	=	144	square inches
1 square yard	=	9	square feet
1 acre	=	43,560	square feet
1 square mile	=	640	acres
10,000 square centimeters	=	1	square meter
10,000 square meters	=	1	hectare
Volume:			
1 cubic foot	=	1,728	cubic inches
1 cubic yard	=	27	cubic feet
1 quart (liquid)	=	2	pints
	=	32	fluid ounces
1 peck	=	8	quarts (dry)
1 bushel	=	4	pecks
	=	32	quarts
1 quart (liquid)	=	0.86	quart (dry)
1 quart (liquid, U.S.)	=	0.83	Imperial Quart
1 gallon	=	4	quarts
1 quart	=	2	pints
	=	946.4	milliliters
1 pint	=	2	cups
1 cup	=	16	tablespoons
	=	2	gills
	=	8	fluid ounces
	=	236.6	milliliters
1 tablespoon	=	3	teaspoons
	=	0.5	fluid ounce
	=	14.8	milliliters
1 teaspoon	=	4.9	milliliters
1 liter	=	1,000	milliliters
	=	1.06	quarts
1,000,000 cubic centimeters	=	1	cubic meter
1,000 milliliters	=	1	liter
1 milliliter	=	1	cubic centimeter

Weight:

1 pound	=	16	ounces
1 ton	=	2,000	pounds
1 long ton	=	2,240	pounds
1 gram	=	0.035	ounces
1 kilogram	=	2.21	pounds
1 ounce	=	28.35	grams
1 pound	=	453.59	grams
1,000 grams	=	1	kilogram
1,000 kilograms	=	1	metric ton

Weights of common building materials

Material	Pounds per cubic foot
Softwood lumber	30–33
Hardwood lumber	35–45
Acrylic plastics	74
Bricks	110–140
Marble	155
Granite	155
Sand or gravel	100
Aluminum	165
Lead	706
Steel and iron	450–485
Portland cement	94
Concrete	145
Glass	160
Coal (piled)	40–58
Hay (baled)	13
Straw (baled)	19
	Pounds per square foot
Acoustical tile	1.0
Linoleum	1.0
Plywood (½-inch)	1.5
Vinyl tile (⅛-inch)	1.4
Asphalt shingles	2.0
Plaster board (½-inch)	10.0
	Pounds per unit
Cement blocks (each)	20–30
2 x 4s, 8 feet long (each)	9–10
½-inch plywood (4-x-8-foot sheet) (each)	50
Asphalt shingles (per bundle)	65

Source: *How to Improve Damn Near Everything Around Your Home*, Peterson and Kesselman-Turkel.

Windchill factor finder

The intersection of registered wind speed and actual thermometer reading is the windchill factor, expressed in degrees. Example: with a wind speed of 10 mph and a temperature of −10° F., the equivalent wind chill temperature is −33° F.

Wind speed (mph)	Actual thermometer reading (° F.)											
	50	40	30	20	10	0	−10	−20	−30	−40	−50	−60
calm	50	40	30	20	10	0	−10	−20	−30	−40	−50	−60
5	48	37	27	16	6	−5	−15	−26	−36	−47	−57	−68
10	40	28	16	4	−9	−21	−33	−46	−58	−70	−83	−95
15	36	22	9	−5	−18	−36	−45	−58	−72	−85	−99	−112
20	32	18	4	−10	−25	−39	−53	−67	−82	−96	−110	−124
25	30	16	0	−15	−29	−44	−59	−74	−88	−104	−118	−133
30	28	13	−2	−18	−33	−48	−63	−79	−94	−109	−125	−140
35	27	11	−4	−20	−35	−49	−67	−82	−98	−116	−129	−145
40	26	10	−6	−21	−37	−53	−69	−85	−100	−118	−132	−148

(Wind speeds greater than 40 mph have little additional effect.)

Source: University of Alaska Extension.

Wind speed estimator

Wind Speed (mph)	Description
Less than 1	Calm. Smoke rises vertically.
1–3	Direction of wind shown by smoke drift but not by wind vanes.
4–7	Wind felt on face; leaves rustle; ordinary vane moved by wind.
8–12	Leaves and small twigs in constant motion; wind extends light flag.
13–18	Raises dust and loose paper; small branches are moved.
19–24	Small trees in leaf begin to sway; crested wavelets form in inland waters.
25–31	Large branches in motion; whistling heard in telephone wires; umbrellas used with difficulty.
32–38	Whole trees in motion; inconvenience felt in walking against wind.

Source: University of Alaska Extension.

Window insulating add-ons

To help stop the flow of heat through windows, many people add ordinary or special drapes, curtains, etc. This chart helps calculate the insulation each feature adds. (R is a measure of insulating value. An inch of Styrofoam is about R 4.)

R value	Window treatment
.06	Loose drapes
.11	Venetian blinds
.15	Drapes fitted to be very tight
.43	Regular window shade
.50	Drapes fitted into airtight edges
.64	Shades sealed to windows bottom and sides
.96	Additional storm window, interior or exterior
1.90	2 additional storm windows
3.0	Insulated Roman shade
4.0	1 inch of Styrofoam fitted tightly into window

Window insulating values

Windows can result in substantial heat loss. This chart compares the relative insulating values of various basic window styles. *U* is an engineering term for how easily any material transmits heat; the lower its figure, the less heat it allows to escape. *R* measures resistance to the escape of heat; the higher its figure, the better its insulating value. For comparison, an inch of fiberglass insulation has an R value of 11; an inch of Styrofoam has an R value of about 4.

	Insulating value	
Type of glazing	**U**	**R**
Single-pane window	1.04	0.96
Double-pane window	0.52	1.92
Double-pane patio door	0.58	1.72
Triple-pane window	0.33	3.03

Source: *How to Improve Damn Near Everything Around Your Home,* Peterson and Kesselman-Turkel.

Wood finishing guide

Finish	Advantages	Disadvantages	Relative cost	Preliminaries for finishing
Lightweight vinyl	Easy to apply. Resists dirt. Easy to clean. Wood and nonwood patterns (marble, burlap, prints, etc.) easy to obtain.	Cuts easily. Won't resist many common solvents. Heat spoils it. Moisture and temperature extremes loosen adhesive. Won't fit on three-dimensional design surfaces.	Moderate	Smooth, clean surfaces with no large blemishes.
Heavyweight vinyl	Very rugged. Wood "grain" is embossed into surface for added realism. Easy to clean. Available in prints, marble pattern, etc.	Heat spoils it. Sensitive to a few volatile solvents.	Expensive	Smooth, clean surfaces with no large blemishes.
Formica-type plastics	Extremely rugged. Very easy to clean. Resists heat and solvents. Available in wood pattern, marble, prints, etc.	Brittle during installation. Not recommended for covering small areas.	Expensive	Smooth, clean surfaces with no large blemishes.
Paint				
Enamel	Rugged. Easy to clean. Resists many common solvents.	Looks amateurish in some uses. Brushes require cleaning in turpentine or benzine.	Inexpensive	Smooth surfaces, well sanded. Primer coat of paint is important. Sandpaper between successive layers.
Water-based	Resists many common solvents. Brushes clean in water.	Looks amateurish in some uses.	Inexpensive	Smooth surfaces, well sanded and well cleaned.

Colored lacquer	Rugged. Easy to clean. Resists many solvents. Looks elegant on modern furniture.	Brushes require solvents for cleaning. Flammable until dry.	Inexpensive	Smooth surfaces, well sanded. Sandpaper between successive layers.
Antique	Rugged. Easy to clean. Resists many common solvents. Looks elegant if well applied.	Takes time to apply. Brushes require solvents to clean in most applications.	Modest	Smooth surfaces, well sanded. Primer is important on bare wood. Can be used on already-painted wood and in some cases to conceal surface defects.
Varnish	Protects natural appearance of real wood. Easy to clean. Relatively rugged.	Brushes require solvent to clean. Doesn't resist water or alcohol well. Dries relatively slowly. Won't stand up under heavy use.	Inexpensive	Smooth surfaces, well sanded. Hardwoods must be treated with filler. Fir plywood may require sealer. Sandpaper or steel wool between successive layers.
Clear lacquer	Rugged. Easy to clean. Resists many common solvents. Looks elegant where clear, shiny look is appropriate. Dries quickly.	Requires solvents to clean brush. Flammable until dry.	Inexpensive	Smooth surfaces, well sanded. Hardwoods must be treated with filler. Fir plywood may require sealer. Sandpaper or steel wool between successive layers.
Clear wood sealer	Very rugged. Easy to clean. Protects wood very deeply. Resists most household hazards except cigarettes. Brings out grain well.	Requires turpentine to clean brush.	Inexpensive	Smooth surfaces, well sanded. Hardwoods must be treated with filler. Sandpaper or steel wool between successive layers. (Often used for several first coats, and then another type of finish such as urethane or varnish is applied.)
Urethane	Very rugged. Protects against almost all household hazards. Easy to clean.	Requires solvent to clean brush.	Modest	Smooth surfaces, well sanded. Hardwoods must be treated with filler. Sandpaper or steel wool between successive layers.

Finish	Advantages	Disadvantages	Relative cost	Preliminaries for finishing
Découpage finish	Each coat is very, very thick and smooth. Provides a smooth covering over rough or uneven areas.	Requires solvent to clean brush. Not as rugged or easy to keep clean as more conventional finishes.	Moderate	Surface does not have to be smooth, but natural woods should be well sanded to show off their grain. A clear wood sealer should be used for one or more preliminary coats to bring out wood grain.
Furniture oil	Beautiful grain and wood. Luxurious "unvarnished" appearance.	Gives wood very little protection against wear or solvents.	Inexpensive	Smooth surfaces, well sanded. Several coats of oil are usually rubbed in with a lot of buffing.
Wax	Easy to apply. Natural, "unvarnished" appearance.	Gives wood very little protection against wear or solvents.	Inexpensive	Smooth surfaces, well sanded. Several coats of oil are usually rubbed in with a lot of buffing.
Shellac	Preserves natural look of wood well. Easy to apply.	Requires alcohol to dilute shellac and clean brush. Minimum resistance to wear, abuse, and solvents or water.	Inexpensive	Smooth surfaces, well sanded. Hardwoods must be treated with filler. Fir plywood must be treated with sealer. Sandpaper or steel wool between coats.
Orange shellac	Often used to provided an instant old-pine look. This effect works best on pine and on fir plywood.	Requires alcohol to dilute shellac and clean brush. Minimum resistance to wear, abuse, and solvents or water.	Inexpensive	Smooth surfaces, well sanded. Hardwoods must be treated with filler. Fir plywood must be treated with sealer. Sandpaper or steel wool between coats.

Source: *The Build-It-Yourself Furniture Catalog*, Peterson.

Woodburning stove and fireplace heating capacities

These figures show the maximum heat that can be derived when operating your woodburner safely, and assume that you begin with thoroughly air-dried wood.

Chimney diameter (in inches)	Wood input (Pounds/hour)	Heat output (BTU/hour)
6	12.1	97,000
7	1.6	131,600
8	21.6	172,400
9	27.3	218,000
10	33.8	270,000

Source: *How to Improve Damn Near Everything Around Your Home,* Peterson and Kesselman-Turkel, based on Underwriters Laboratory tests.

Cross-Reference Guide

Gardening

Hardware

Health

Home improvements

Household management

Money management

Numbers

Outdoors